# Contents

# Preface

**M**any listeners of the *Voice of Prophecy* radio broadcast have sacrificed time to write and send us a description of their experiences with angels. Some of the testimonies were so gripping that we at the Voice of Prophecy offices contacted those listeners for more details. We believe that you will be inspired and encouraged by these compelling accounts of angels who walk with us in our day.

Let me share with you the amazing story behind this book. It began with my previous angel book, *In the Presence of Angels*, coauthored with Timothy Crosby in 1995.

Several years ago at a Christian Booksellers Association convention in Chicago, representatives of Pacific Press® rented a booth just across the hall from *Guideposts* magazine's display. The *Guideposts* representative ambled over to the Pacific Press® booth in search of the recently published account of a handicapped mountain climber (*More Than Mountains: The Todd Huston Story* by Todd Huston with Kay Rizzo), a book he had wanted to read. While perusing the display he saw our book, *In the Presence of Angels*. Immediately it seized his attention. He knew that a leading national book club was looking for a new collection of true angel stories and wanted *Guideposts'* assistance in finding such a work right away. Movies and TV series like *Touched by an Angel, Highway to Heaven,* and *Angels in the Outfield* were taking America by storm. Along with the popularity of these shows was a steadily widening demand for printed matter on angels.

Sensing his opportunity, the *Guideposts* representative obtained a copy of our book and took it to his publication board. "This is the book we need," they concluded. *Guideposts* worked out a contract with Pacific Press® to acquire second publication rights. Soon, more than 40,000 beautifully illustrated hardback copies of the book rolled off their presses and were sent to book club subscribers. It became the Book of the Month for May 1996. Thus our book was given a new set of wings that landed it in many thousands of homes across North America. A miracle of divine timing and Spirit-led opportunity!

Much to our disappointment, however, the publisher omitted an indispensable chapter entitled "Masquerade." We wrote that chapter to help readers guard against being lured into the many false concepts of angels that have ensnared millions of unsuspecting people in the mesh of spiritism. In *Walking with Angels* we have revisited the dark side of the supernatural in the chapter called "Evil Angels." Here you will read the warnings from God's Holy Word on how to avoid being deceived by demonic impersonators of heaven's angels. In this age of satanically crafted miracles that take the form of apparitions, cosmic gurus, and supposed spirits of the dead, none of us can afford to be without God's instruction on this subject. But even more important, He would not have us ignorant of the way of salvation in Jesus. Everything that heaven does, whether seemingly ordinary or miraculous, is designed to prepare us for present duty and future glory.

The age of divine miracles has not ended. And the age of God's loving interest in our lives will never end, but will continue throughout all ages for the redeemed. Meanwhile, I pray that *Walking with Angels* will spark positive developments in your life by drawing you into a closer walk with God. Share this book with loved ones; it may bring them special courage and guidance for these challenging days. I hope that you will enjoy reading this collection of angel stories as much as I did in selecting and retelling them with assistance from my friend, Pastor Brian Jones.

Your own story may be just what's needed to give someone the courage to endure tragedy and trial and gain fresh hope for tomorrow. Please contact us at the Voice of Prophecy and tell us what this book has meant to you when you finish reading it. We'd also love to hear your angel story. You may write to us at gospel@vop.com or Voice of Prophecy, Box 53055, Los Angeles, CA 90053.

Maranatha!

E. Lonnie Melashenko

# Introduction

ave you ever wondered, "Why all the interest in angels in today's world?" Stories abound about people's experiences with angels. Often it doesn't seem to matter if those who have these experiences are at all spiritual or if the subjects' lives change significantly from their encounter with angels. We're almost at the point where it's become embarrassing to be without one's own personal angel story. "You mean, you haven't seen an angel yet? What's the matter with you?"

But the un-angeled who have missed meeting one of these celestial celebrities may take comfort in buying angel T-shirts, angel figurines, angel chocolates, angel calendars, angel necklaces, angel dolls, angel stationery, angel cards—and angel books. Or they may watch TV programs, such as *Touched by an Angel*. Has the whole subject become commercialized and trivialized? Has the popularity of angels so saturated the market and airwaves that we have become glutted with the subject and are ready to turn to some new fad?

The authors of this book think that from the perspective of God's Word, most people in our culture have been given a distorted and misleading view of angels. Clouds of hype, trivia, and fantasy surround this subject today that have as much relevance to the real meaning of angels as Easter bunnies and bonnets have to do with the resurrection of Jesus.

Think about it from the standpoint of the Bible's last book, Revelation. In this book, the apostle John describes the wrap-up of human history leading up to Christ's second coming. Revelation is a short book. You can read it (if you don't stop very long to ponder its meaning) in about 20 minutes. But in this brief, fascinating account of things past, present, and future, you will find more than 75 references to angels! In Revelation you will find angels bearing messages to the whole world; angels holding back winds of war and strife; angels carrying out missions of divine judgment; angels engaged in cosmic war; angels traveling at quantum speeds between heaven and earth; angels singing songs of praise; angels giving glory to God; and angels refusing worship.

This book proposes to answer some questions about angels. Who are they? What is their connection with humanity? What are their main activities? Are there evil angels as well as good ones? How can you tell the difference? Do I have a guardian angel? Can I communicate with him? What part will angels play in my future? What part do they play in my life now?

It is the aim of this book to answer these questions and others just as important to you. We offer these answers from God's Word in the setting of *some of the most amazing true angel stories that have taken place in the history of the world*, from Bible times to our day. So, prepare yourself as we take off on a flight to realms far more amazing, relevant, and real than any that science-fiction writers and fable-makers have imagined in their most dazzling dreams and daring moments.

# Walking with Angels

More True Stories From the Author of
*In the Presence of Angels*

# E. Lonnie Melashenko
# with Brian D. Jones

**Pacific Press® Publishing Association**
Nampa, Idaho
Oshawa, Ontario, Canada

Edited by Tim Lale
Designed by Dennis Ferree
Cover photo by Kamil Vojnar/Photonica®

ISBN: 0-8163-1785-2

00 01 02 03 04 • 5 4 3 2 1

# CHAPTER ONE

# *Angel Deliverers*

John Wesley was probably as proper and conservative an Englishman as you'd ever meet. He was not a radical or revolutionary, at least not from our modern perspective. But he had the Church of England as shaken up as if he were the Antichrist in clerical robes.

Wesley was not brash, fanatical, or unscrupulous, nor was he a disturber of the peace. In fact he was a benefactor to the poor, imprisoned, and oppressed. And yet when Wesley came to town, the church authorities would declare war against him and his helpers.

You see, Wesley preached the gospel of Scripture. His teachings were similar to those found in the book of Acts. And he produced the same results as did the apostles—he shook up the regular order of things to make way for truths that turn the world upside down (see Acts 4:13-33; 17:6).

So disturbingly biblical were Wesley's teachings that, although he was an ordained Anglican minister, he was compelled to do most of his preaching outdoors and in chapels especially erected for meetings—meetings that the established church strongly desperately feared. Wesley's supporters, who had become known as Methodists, were persecuted for their efforts. Sometimes priests incited mobs to break up the meetings and rough up the Methodist preachers.

In 1746 Wesley went to the city of Falmouth to visit a sick man. While in Falmouth Wesley held some meetings, which aroused the indignation of those who wanted to remain comfortable in the practice of their fashionable sins. Hearing that Wesley was at the sick man's house, a mob went in search of the preacher to beat him up, and if he should die in the process, then England would be rid of an arch-heretic, as far as they were concerned.

Gathering in front of the house, they shouted, "Where is the Methodist? We want the Methodist."

Wesley did not come out, so the mob decided to break into the house. Knocking down the door, they rushed inside and charged up the stairs. When they reached the bedroom, they found that the door was locked. The men in front held back. But some sailors bustled forward saying, "Avast, lads, avast!" These burly men were little better than pirates and gloried in a fight. Taking turns, several of these sailors flung their bulky weight against the door, and after a few batterings the door fell down with its hinges flying off.

There was nothing now between them and the man they so blindly hated—nothing, that is, except the angels and the power of God.

Wesley arose from the chair where he had been sitting and, looking steadily into the men's eyes, said, "Here I am. Did one of you want to talk to me?" The angry men stood still. Their roaring and shouting died away. As Wesley, who was five feet tall and weighed scarcely 100 pounds, walked forward, the men fell back. Wesley advanced into the upper passageway, and the mobsters pressed themselves against the wall to give him room to pass. All through the passageway and down the stairs, the attackers pressed against wall and railing as though an unseen force were pushing them aside. With glowering eyes and murder in their hearts, they watched Wesley, but they could not lift a foot or a fist against him.

As Wesley made his way through the hostile crowd, he spoke calmly to them, reproving them for their hatefulness and challenging them to give one reason for their wicked behavior.

Hundreds of men blocked the door outside and filled the street, but they too were compelled to make way for the diminutive Wesley, who was a giant in the faith and a champion of truth rarely seen in any age. God commissioned angels to protect the life of His valiant servant.

❧ ❧ ❧ ❧

Does God send angels to protect His servants in our own time? During a revolutionary period a few years ago in an African country that is still in political turmoil, Mike Pearson served as pastor in a large district situated in the midst of the conflict. Three times a week he had to drive on a main highway where the traffic was sparse because of guerrilla activity. Anybody who traveled that way was subject to being killed without cause. But Pastor Mike was faithful, and several times a week for about two years he drove along this road to fulfill his pastoral duties.

Finally the day came when the two sides declared a truce, and a shaky peace returned to that African country. One day Pastor Mike had some official business to conduct at a government office. After completing his errand, he came out of the building and was astonished to be greeted by a tall man in military dress, with bandoleers and grenades attached to his uniform. With a genial smile the soldier said to Pastor Pearson, "Sir, I'd like to shake your hand."

Pastor Mike is a friendly person, but this approach from such a stranger took him by surprise. So he answered, "Oh, why would you like to do that?"

The soldier replied, "I'd like to shake the hand of the man we could not kill."

Pastor Mike said, "Please explain."

"Did you not used to travel on the main highway every Monday, Wednesday, and Thursday and pass the midpoint at about 10:00 A.M. on those days in your brown Toyota wagon?"

"Yes," Pastor Mike answered, his curiosity rising.

"Well, sir, on seven different occasions my fellow guards and I tried to kill you. Our plan was to shoot you as you drove by. Each time you came along, we had you clearly in sight from our post in the bush, but our guns refused to work when we pressed the triggers. As soon as you drove out of range, the guns would work again. We carefully tested our AK 47's before and after your passing through that way, and they worked flawlessly. But then they simply would not fire when we directed them at you. It could only have been a spirit or an angel that kept our guns from working. So, that's why I'd like to shake your hand. God is on your side—or you are on His!"

What a strange experience it must have been for Pastor Pearson to shake the hand of his would-be assassin! But how gratifying for him to know that he was under the care of angels even when he was oblivious of danger.

"He shall give His angels charge over you, to keep you in all your ways."

Two opposite reasons have made this perhaps the most famous angel verse in the Bible. The first is that it comes from the 91st Psalm, which God's people have treasured for thousands of years. The second reason is that Satan tried to make deceptive use of this verse when tempting Jesus in the wilderness. He wanted the Savior to presume on God's protecting care by jumping off the pinnacle of the temple, and thereby challenge His Father to give Him a safe landing. Jesus would never allow Himself to be lured into "daring" God to prove His Word. Not only did Satan misapply this verse when presenting it to Jesus as an excuse for recklessly endangering His life, but he also misquoted it. Satan omitted the words "in all your ways." God will keep us safe and secure when *our ways* harmonize with *His way.*

❦ ❦ ❦ ❦

On a bitterly cold day in January 1940, the car taking the Thomas family into London crept along the slippery road. In spite of constant movement, the windshield wipers could not keep the window clear of the snow that was falling thick and fast. Several times Pastor Thomas stopped the car and brushed the snow away. It was nearly dark when the family finally reached the railway station where they would take the train to the channel port of Folkestone. From there they would cross to France.

The Thomas family had been on furlough for a year from Kenya, in east Africa. During that fateful year, England and its empire had been plunged into the horrors of World War II. Although no bombs had yet fallen on Britain, many ships had been sunk in the waters surrounding the island. Because of the dangers of sea travel, church leaders had decided that the returning missionary family should go from France to Italy by train, then take a neutral ship to the east African port of Mombasa.

Pastor and Mrs. Thomas and their four sons, ranging in age from three to thirteen, stood in the pitch blackness of the railway station, holding onto their suitcases, and waiting for the train to come.

The blackout was a serious matter in those days. Civil authorities allowed no lights of any kind that might be seen from the air.

The Thomas family heard, rather than saw, the coaches as they came to a stop in front of them. Tightly holding hands, the Thomases boarded the train. Five hundred soldiers also got on. The doors slammed, the guard blew his whistle, and the train slowly pulled out of the station.

How strange it felt to be riding along in the blackness of night! Conversations were going on all around them, but they could not see a single soul. Some of the soldiers were singing, some were cursing the war that had taken them from their homes and families. The minutes seemed to pass slowly as the rails clicked off the miles.

Noses pressed against the window, the Thomas boys could see

no friendly lights from farmhouses, nor from any of the villages they passed through. Even the ground, though covered with snow, could hardly be seen in the gloom. After what seemed like hours, the train began to slow down as it neared the seacoast where the steamer was waiting to take them across the English Channel to France.

Once again Pastor Thomas reminded the boys to keep together, hold hands, and follow him. The train stopped, and hundreds of passengers poured onto the platform, the Thomas family among them. But where were they to go? An icy wind blew around them as they stood, bewildered. Suddenly a tall man appeared out of the darkness.

"Follow me," he said. "I know where you must go."

Down the platform they followed his dimly visible form. He led them through a dark room into another that was well lighted. For a few minutes all they could do was blink, the lights seemed so bright. Then they saw that this was the room where officials would examine their passports and luggage. They turned to look at their guide and saw that he was a tall man dressed in a heavy brown overcoat.

The man led them to a table where an officer sat ready to inspect their passports. The officer asked whether Pastor Thomas was carrying any letters. During the war, military officials would very carefully inspect all letters leaving or entering England to see that they contained no important information that might help the enemy. Pastor Thomas admitted that he was carrying some letters, and at the request of the officer, he laid them on the table.

The letters had been written by former Adventist missionaries in Kenya, and Pastor Thomas was carrying them to African people whom the missionaries had known. They were all written in Luo, an African language. This was very serious indeed because no one in that room could read and translate the letters except Pastor Thomas himself, and the officer said that he could not accept Pastor Thomas's word.

Just then the man in the brown coat spoke up. "These are missionaries," he said. "I know them, and I know that there is nothing in those letters dangerous to our country."

"Very well," said the officer, "we will let them pass."

Pastor Thomas looked at the stranger in surprise. Where had this man ever known the Thomas family? When had he read those letters? It was very mysterious. Pastor Thomas expressed his gratitude to him. The man did not answer but proceeded to help them out of another difficulty.

All over the room, customs officers were examining luggage. They were taking no chances. One of the officials came to Pastor Thomas and indicated that he wanted the luggage opened for inspection. Pastor Thomas had not expected this. Ordinarily, British subjects traveling in peacetime did not have their luggage inspected when going from one part of the empire to another. Knowing this, and not stopping to think of the difference wartime might make, he had strapped up his suitcases very thoroughly. The idea of opening them all now filled him with dismay.

The man in the brown coat spoke up again.

"These people are missionaries," he told the inspector. "I can vouch for their luggage. It does not contain anything prohibited by law."

"Very well," said the officer briskly, and motioned them toward the door leading to the gangplank.

A few minutes later the family had climbed aboard the ship. Dim lights burned here and there in the long corridors. One of the stewards came to meet them. He explained that the soldiers had taken almost all the beds on board, but he did have a few places for the ladies. He asked Mrs. Thomas to follow him.

Mrs. Thomas shook her head. "No, I am not going to be separated from my husband. If this ship is going to be torpedoed, the whole family will go down together." Seeing she was determined to stay with her husband and their boys, the steward shrugged his shoulders and went on his way.

Almost instinctively Pastor Thomas turned to the man in the

brown coat. For the third time, he did not fail them.

"I know a place for you," he said. "It is not an ideal place for a missionary family to sleep, but at least you will not be disturbed."

He led them to the ship's bar. It was after midnight, and the bar was closed. Around the room by the walls were leather-padded benches. On these, the family could lie down and rest for the remainder of the night.

Pastor Thomas pushed the suitcases one by one under the benches. Then he turned to thank the tall stranger once more for all his kindness. But he was gone! Stepping quickly into the hall, Pastor Thomas looked up and down the passage. He could see no sign of the man. He went to the top of the gangplank and asked the officers there whether they had seen the man in the brown coat.

"There wasn't anyone like that on the boat tonight," they replied. "If there had been, we would have seen him."

Yet Pastor Thomas knew there had been such a man, for he had talked with him. But now he had disappeared into the night.

He returned to the barroom and reported to his family. "It must have been an angel," said Mrs. Thomas softly.[1]

❦ ❦ ❦ ❦

Nick and Claudia P., a couple from Nebraska, signed up to serve as English teachers in a city in northern China. During their first tour of duty they taught at the provincial university and lived in a "Foreign Expert Building," where they could be kept under the ever-watchful eyes of officialdom. Between university students in the daytime and government workers in the evening, Nick and Claudia taught about 500 students each week. In this city of 6 million, there are fewer than 50 Americans at any one time.

On Thanksgiving Day, 1993, Nick and Claudia were scheduled to start class with a new group of students. The classroom assigned for their use was cold and bleak. Sharp Siberian winds knifed through the loosely hinged windows to kill whatever warmth might accumulate from the people gathered in the room. Claudia tells the rest of the story in her own words:

"In class, after enrolling and designating English names to this diverse group, I decided to tell a story and test our students' listening comprehension. I told them the story of Pollyanna. They loved the idea of learning to play the 'Glad Game' and to hunt for something in every situation to be glad about. We were glad that putting smiles on our faces, even here in China, could melt frozen hearts and smooth the way for us to make forever friends.

" 'Dear Jesus,' I prayed, 'please give us a sign that You're in this place and that You still care for us.'

"For the last half of our class we had free talk. The students really liked that time. We divided the class into two sections. I moved my group to the top part of the room. The students circled closely around each of us so we could talk and listen together. Below and to my left I could hear them asking Nick questions about his Christianity and if he really believed and accepted Jesus as his personal Savior. I was proud of him for speaking boldly about his faith even though he recognized the danger. This is not America. Religious freedom is different here from the way it is in our homeland. But questions of the heart need to be answered.

"My group talked about other things. They asked me to sing for them, so I taught them 'Over the River and Through the Woods' and 'Jesus Loves the Little Children, All the Children of the World.' I thought of our new granddaughter and the Thanksgiving celebrations going on back home. Meanwhile, our three communist guards looked on with stony faces, and I became concerned over our boldness in talking about Jesus.

"Suddenly an older man, dressed in a soldier's overcoat, stepped very close to my face and asked, 'Who is the tall, American-looking boy that always goes everywhere with you when you go out?'

"There are no Americans anywhere in the area where we live. He could see Nick in our classroom, so he knew the 'boy' he asked about wasn't my husband. I couldn't think of whom he might mean. And then the question went around the circle, with others asking the same thing. In various levels of English and in sometimes difficult-to-understand accents, many of them asked, 'Yes, who is the tall American boy that goes with you? We have seen him with you as you walk from class to class and when you are headed out the campus gates to go shopping.'

"I had no answer. Any boys who go with us in China look very Chinese—and most of them are short!

"I came home from class still wondering, but as I awoke in the morning the answer came to me. Many years ago when I was just a little girl I remember my dear Auntie Ruth teaching me the Good News of Psalm 34:7.

"I prayed, 'Oh, Thank You God, for the *best* Thanksgiving ever!'

"I'm not sure just what a guardian angel looks like, but I feel convinced that mine looks like a tall American boy and has been seen by many Chinese eyes. And I believe that God provided 'a tall American boy' to hold the door open for the entrance of gospel light."[2]

❦ ❦ ❦ ❦

Angels need not always be visible in order to be evident. One of the world's greatest champions of liberty, Roger Williams, never reported having seen an angel. Nonetheless, he was keenly aware of the role of divine providence in sparing him from death at the hands of Puritan persecutors, who could not tolerate Williams's ideas of freedom and purity of worship. W. A. Spicer, in his book, *The Hand That Intervenes,* indicates the work of angels behind the scenes in Roger Williams's life. Spicer writes:

"It was in the dead of winter, in the year 1635, that Roger Williams fled from Salem, having been banished from the Massachusetts Bay Colony for his defense of liberty of conscience. He was alone in the New England wilds. 'I was sorely tossed for fourteen weeks,' he wrote, in a bitter winter season, not knowing what bread or bed did mean.'

"All his life long he carried the lively remembrance that God indeed helped him and delivered him. He saw the intervening providence of God in influencing the governor of the Massachusetts Bay Colony to help him privately in getting away, and the hand of God also in turning the hearts of the wild Indians toward him. Thirty-five years after his flight, he wrote to his friend Mason:

"Governor Mr. Winthrop privately wrote to me to steer my course to Narragansett Bay and Indians, for many high and heavenly and public ends encouraging me, from the freeness of the place from any English claims or patents. I took his prudent motion as a hint and voice from God, and waiving all other thoughts and motions, I steered my course from Salem (though in winter snow, which I feel yet) unto those parts, wherein I may say 'Peniel,' that is, I have seen the face of *God.—Letters Vol. VI, p. 335.*

"He felt that as truly as God sent food to Elijah by the ravens, so He had sent succor to him by the Indians of the forest wilds. Dropping into verse, he wrote:

*"God's providence is rich to His;*
*Let none distrustful be;*
*In wilderness, in great distress,*
*These ravens have fed me.*

"And continuing in song his story of delivering providence, he bore testimony:

*"God makes a path, provides a guide,*
*And feeds in wilderness!*
*His glorious name, while breath remains,*
*O that I may confess!*

*"Lost many a time, I've had no guide,*
*No house but hollow tree!*
*In stormy winter night no fire,*
*No food, no company.*

*"In Him I found a house, a bed,*
*A table, company!*
*No cup so bitter, but's made sweet,*
*When God shall sweet'ning be.*
    —"Key into the Language of America."*

"Well may we know that angels of God went with him; for Roger Williams was the agent in God's providence for the first planting of the standard of full religious liberty in the New World."[3]

❧ ❧ ❧ ❧

We might find it relatively easy to believe that angels would protect a mighty champion of religious liberty like Roger Williams. But what about an unknown farm girl on the plains of Alberta, Canada? Have you ever thought of angels' wings serving as a tent or canopy to protect God's praying children? Here is Alma W.'s story, which she sent to the Voice of Prophecy in response to a request for true angel stories.

"I am 80 years old, but I wish to relate an experience that took place when I was around 13 or 14, which I recall as though it just happened yesterday.

"My father was blind. He felt it was useless to rent pasture for our horses when they could be of use on Brother and Sister Hughes's farm near Didsbury, Alberta, about 8 miles south of Olds.

"It was a difficult task for me to harness them, though it was my job. Rudolph was a big horse for me to put the collar and harness on. I had to stand on a crate to do it. Daisy was less trouble.

"Around noon I finally started out. We lived in the south end of Olds. I needed to go north one block to cross the railway tracks and then west one mile, then south.

"I enjoyed the scenery as we passed a field of barley, ready to be harvested. Then I heard a strange rumbling sound in the west. I had not noticed dark clouds or any indication of trouble. Then I saw it. Thick sheets of hail were rapidly advancing toward us eastward across the field. We could hear the hail bouncing and battering as it approached.

"Rudolph and Daisy were flighty horses, so I expected trouble. As I saw the hail coming, I prayed that the Lord would protect the horses. I feared Dad's wrath over any damage we might suffer, so indirectly I was praying for myself, too.

"Then the hail struck all around us, and I cringed, expecting to be hurt. But not a pellet struck us. I looked at the horses, which trotted along as if everything was normal. Then I looked at my feet, and in the back of the wagon, but there was not one hailstone, though we were now surrounded by the storm, rushing and rattling like a barrage of ice bullets.

"Then I looked up. The hail came to a point, then parted as if we were in a tent, and I praised God for His divine protection. Though I held the reins in my hands I knew I was not controlling the horses.

"Then another thought struck me, and I again sent up a prayer. We were approaching the railway crossing, and the 12:30 passenger train coming into Olds was due about then. I could not see anything because of the hail, and its noise prevented me from hearing the train whistle. We bumped over the tracks, and then I noticed the dark form of the engine approaching behind us. It roared past moments after our crossing.

"With tears coursing down my cheeks, I praised our great Protector and had a story to tell when I arrived at Brother and Sister Hughes's home. We all praised God together.

"The next day when I returned, that beautiful field of barley was pounded into the ground as though it had been turned by a disc. Lightning had splintered a power pole. I still don't understand why dark clouds or other warnings of a hailstorm had not appeared. When I get to heaven I want to learn what ingenious method the angel used to spare us from harm that day. Meanwhile, this experience has helped me through some difficult times."[4]

❦ ❦ ❦ ❦

Truly our lives are interwoven with those of angels. This is especially true of those who love God and wish to serve Him faithfully, as an expression of gratitude for His salvation. "For the eyes of the Lord run to and fro throughout the whole earth, to show Himself strong on behalf of those whose heart is loyal to Him" (2 Chronicles 16:9). And often He mediates that strength through His angels, who are always ready to do His bidding.

Ardythe Hovland of Hawaii tells the story of her father-in-law, Halvor Hovland. This story has greatly strengthened the Hovland family's faith down through the years. Ardythe herself heard it from Halvor.

In the early 1900s the Hovland family moved to a farm near Eldon, Missouri. Some time during this period, Halvor had an experience that he loved to recount with awe. It was harvest time, and in those days farmers cut their grain with a scythe. One cloudy Friday afternoon, when the grain was perfectly ripe, Mr. Fogelman, a neighbor, came over and said, "Halvor, you'll have to cut your crop tomorrow, or it will go down on you."

From a farmer's standpoint Mr. Fogelman's words made sense. For, when the grain becomes over-ripe, the weight of the heads makes it lie down flat in the field, thus making it impossible to reap. An entire crop can be lost this way.

Halvor's reply was, "Well, it will just have to 'go down' then, Mr. Fogelman, because tomorrow is Saturday, the seventh-day Sabbath, and the fourth commandment tells us to do no work on that day. I'll trust in God and harvest my grain the next day."

Fogelman's reply was, "You're crazy, man! It is cloudy now, and by tomorrow it might even rain. You'd better get an early start tomorrow morning, Sabbath or no Sabbath." But Halvor remained firm in his convictions; he prayed that the storm clouds would pass over and that the ripened grain would remain standing until Sunday.

His prayer was answered, and all day Sunday he worked under the hot sun, cutting swath after swath of grain with his scythe. He hardly stopped to rest and by nightfall, instead of getting only one-half the crop harvested, he was surprised to find that he had been able to cover the entire field!

When he went to the house, he told his wife, Carrie, that he was very thankful to have the crop all cut and was amazed that he had been able to do so much in just one day.

On Monday morning, Mr. Fogelman was back again. "Well, Halvor, I see you got all your grain cut. But where did you find someone to help you on a Sunday? You know we're all strict Sunday-keepers around here, and I didn't know of anyone available for hire on that day."

Halvor said, "What do you mean? No one helped me. I did it all by myself."

Fogelman said, "Now, Halvor, I've always known you as a man of your word and you have never lied to me in all the years you've lived here, so don't start now. You know good and well that it takes two days to cut that field of grain, and here it is all done in one day. Now tell me, who did you get to help you?"

Halvor again replied, "No one, I'm telling you. No one helped me."

By this time, Mr. Fogelman was puzzled and said, "Halvor, I know what I saw. There was a man who followed you all day long. He walked right behind you. I watched him from my kitchen window. He had a scythe just like yours, and when you cut a swath, he would cut a swath. When you stopped to clean your scythe, he would stop and clean his scythe. When you stopped to rest, he would stop."

Halvor loved to tell this story to his children and grandchildren and would always finish by reading this verse in the Bible: "The angel of the Lord encamps around those who fear Him" (Psalm 34:7, NASB).

He also often quoted Isaiah 58:13, 14: "If because of the sabbath, you turn your foot from doing your own pleasure on My
holy day, and call the sabbath a delight, the holy day of the Lord
honorable, and shall honor it, desisting from your own ways,
from seeking your own pleasure, and speaking your own word,
then you will take delight in the Lord, and I will make you ride
on the heights of the earth; and I will feed you with the heritage
of Jacob your father, for the mouth of the Lord has spoken"
(NASB).[5]

❦ ❦ ❦ ❦

Carol H. of Delta Junction, Alaska, tells the story of how
angels brought triumph out of tragedy in her life. Carol writes:

"On July 25,1992, my husband and I had traveled 100 miles to
Fairbanks, Alaska, to pick up my parents, who were coming for
a visit. Even though we were driving home a little after midnight,
it was still light. The sun had just dipped below the horizon.

"About 15 miles from home we were driving through a
swampy area with a slight drop-off on the right side of the road
when suddenly a moose sprang onto the road. I don't think my
husband even got his foot off the accelerator. It felt as though we
hit a brick wall. Then I was aware of a tremendous weight in my
lap. I slowly opened my eyes—it was the windshield.

"Except for a cut on my arm, I was OK. My husband was killed
instantly. We were driving a small Saab with a sunroof that was
slightly open at the time. The front of the car apparently knocked
the moose off its feet, and it landed on the strip of the roof
between the top of the windshield and the sunroof, and that strip
of metal crashed into the front seat, hitting my husband's head.

"A couple of weeks later, the smashed car was towed to my
house and left out by the garage. In my attempt to make some
sense out of the greatest tragedy of my life, I went out to examine the car. I swept away enough glass to sit once again in the
passenger's seat and saw something that made me think that
there may really be a God. The strip of metal that had come
crashing in, killing my husband, had conformed around my head

without the slightest contact. From where I was sitting in that car, there was only about an inch of space where the metal had wrapped itself around my head.

"Even then, in my pagan mindset, the only explanation I could think of was that an angel had reached down and put his hand in front of my face, and the metal just went around.

"Now, all these years later, I have no doubt this is what happened. God had to take drastic measures to reach me, and it worked.

"I am now a leader in my local church, and my son was baptized two years ago in the Jordan River and is now a sophomore at Walla Walla College [in Washington State]. Considering my negative attitude toward Christianity when my son was young, this is truly a miracle.

"I pray that someday I can thank that angel face to face. As I think back on my life, it took the death of two men to save me—Jesus' for my salvation, and my husband's, to bring me to a point of openness to Christ for salvation and relief from pain."

Truly, as Isaiah said, "In all their affliction He was afflicted, and the angel of His presence saved them; in His love and in His mercy He redeemed them; and He lifted them and carried them all the days of old" (Isaiah 63:9, NASB).[6]

❦ ❦ ❦ ❦

The following experience, related by evangelist A. S. Rodd, of England, shows what the Lord does sometimes to lead honest hearts into the light. Pastor Rodd writes:

"Some years ago a lady came to our evangelistic meetings. She had been an invalid, scarcely able to walk. Though an earnest Christian, she was dissatisfied with her past experience, and longing to find the way of truth more fully. To this end she had prayed.

"One night in a dream, she told us, it seemed to her that an angel came and spoke to her. In the dream she said to the angel: 'I do not see how you can find the time to come to me.'

"Her visitant replied: 'I can spare time always to visit anyone who wants the truth.'

"He beckoned her to follow and led her to a mission hall, and pointing her to a certain seat in the hall, he asked her to listen here and receive the truth. 'You will find the truth here,' the angel said. Then she awoke.

" 'Ever since,' she said to us, 'I have looked for that mission hall.'

"Long had she searched up and down the city, visiting one place and then another, without finding the hall of which she had so vivid an impression.

" 'But here I see it tonight,' she said, 'and there,' pointing to a certain chair, 'is the very place where I sat in my dream.' Needless to say, she was an attentive listener as the meetings continued, and with joy she accepted fully the message for these times."

God knows every home in all the great cities where someone is praying for light. If all the angels are "ministering spirits, sent out to render service for the sake of those who will inherit salvation" (Hebrews 1:14, NASB), why should we doubt that an angel would visit a praying soul and point the way to the place of truth?

---

1. Adapted from *Only In Africa*, by Virgil E. Robinson (Review and Herald, 1965), pp. 97-101.
2. From Claudia and Nicholas Parks, Lincoln, Nebraska
3. From *The Hand that Intervenes*, by W. A. Spicer (Review and Herald, 1918), pp. 40, 41.
4. From Alma Wells, Kelowna, BC, Canada
5. From Ms. Ardythe Hovland, Aiea, Hawaii
6. From Carol Holley, Delta Junction, Alaska

# CHAPTER TWO

# Angel Comforters

Susan and Mary, two beautiful teenage sisters, lived in rural South Dakota in the early 1890s. They had recently given their hearts to Jesus at an evangelistic meeting held in a big tent just after harvest season. Life then was very much different from what we know today in the dawn of a new millennium, and it wasn't always idyllic.

In fact, for Mary and Susan, life had suddenly grown very difficult. It had to do with their newfound walk with Jesus.

Much to their mother Margaret's disgust, the sisters had begun faithfully attending church every Sabbath. Margaret tried everything she could think of to dissuade the girls from keeping the Sabbath and attending church. Living at home became more and more miserable for the two girls as their mother resorted to threats, commands, and unkind treatment to draw them away from their new faith.

The girls' most precious possession was a little black

pocket Bible that they read secretly for comfort and strength. Their mother became infuriated because Susan and Mary had turned so "fanatical" through the influence of that book. So they read in secret each evening in bed. Time and again the sharp-eared girls foiled their mother's surprise visits to catch them in the act of reading the Bible. A creak of the floor outside their room, and in a flash the Bible disappeared under the pillow or bed cover. The girls feared that if their mother found their Bible she would throw it in the flames of the kitchen stove.

One day the floor didn't creak, and they were caught avidly poring over the cherished Word. Furiously, Margaret snatched the Bible and destroyed it in just the way her daughters had feared.

Attempting to make the girls forget their "strange" beliefs, Margaret sent Susan away to learn the trade of hat making. Mary, now alone at home, became so miserable that she finally moved to another town, where some kindly Christian friends took her in.

When summer came, Margaret brought Susan home again, but without Mary the pressure seemed too great to bear alone. Susan wrote letters to Mary begging her to return. Soon they were happily reunited. As the weeks passed the two girls often walked five miles to church and Sabbath School.

Few bright spots lightened their tension-filled home, but secretly, Susan was busy making the "perfect hat" for herself. Giving every detail special attention, she decreed that no one was to see the hat until she had gotten it just right. Finally one Friday afternoon, Susan appeared in the doorway of the kitchen. "How do you like my new hat, Mother?" she asked, pleased with her creative achievement.

Glancing up from her bread making, Margaret asked, "What special occasion calls for such an elegant hat?"

Susan smiled. "It is to be my Sabbath hat, Mother, I'll wear it for the first time tomorrow."

A dark, angry look crossed Margaret's face. She stepped across the room, snatched the hat from Susan's head, and tore it in pieces. Stung to the very depths, Susan raced from the kitchen and across the field to the family orchard. "How could a mother be so cruel to a girl who was trying to live the best possible life?" she asked herself, as hot tears welled up in her eyes. It seemed that all hope was snatched from her. Had God forgotten two young girls who had given all to Him?

That night, as the girls crawled into their beds in the attic bedroom, Susan began to shake with deep, uncontrollable sobs. Mary tried to comfort Susan but felt too empty and forlorn herself to offer much help. Together, the sisters wept and cried to God for support in their hour of despair.

Suddenly Mary sat up in bed, astonished. "Do you see it, Susan?" The small attic bedroom was filled with a rich, warm light. The two huddled closer together.

"What can this mean?" Susan asked.

"Do you suppose it's an angel?" Mary whispered.

"Hush, I'm going to find out what this is," Susan replied as she tiptoed out of bed. She peered out the window and down through the hole where the stovepipe came through the ceiling, but everywhere she looked outside of their room was inky blackness. The light continued to shine a mellow glow that brought a special comfort in the darkness of the girls' despondency.

"Mary, do you think God has sent an angel to give us some hope of happiness in the future? Some sign that we aren't entirely alone, and that He has not forsaken us?" Susan asked.

Mary could not answer. All she could do was squeeze Susan's hand. As the light shone on, a marvelous comforting peace filled their hearts, and soon they were lost in tranquil slumber. Echoing in their minds was their Savior's promise: "I will never leave you nor forsake you."

In the morning the peace remained. The two girls eagerly dressed and hurried down to tell their mother what had happened, certain that she would rejoice with them over this wonderful experience. Their hopes were abruptly dashed. Margaret forbade the girls ever to mention again such foolish imaginings. "The very idea!" she snorted, "angels coming to comfort you.

How could you girls be so proud and silly?"

Years passed before Margaret joined her daughters in their deep commitment to God's Word. But the encouragement they received that night when an angel came to strengthen them in drinking the cup of scorned discipleship gave the sisters courage to continue in the path they had chosen. Mary and Susan became remarkable witnesses for Jesus in countries where His name was little known. As a result of their labors, hundreds of people who were living in darkness came to see the Light that guided the pathway of these two brave missionaries.[1]

❧ ❧ ❧ ❧

Angels are experts in giving encouragement to God's tried children who are persecuted for their faith, no matter how dire the circumstances. If we go back many centuries, we find Ruffinus, a historian, who tells the story of Theodorus, a witness who suffered extreme torture at the hands of Julian the Apostate. In his determination to make him deny Christ, Julian subjected Theodorus to torture that was humanly unendurable.

Years after this dreadful ordeal, Ruffinus met Theodorus and asked the faithful sufferer, "How could you possibly stand the pain of all that relentless torture?"

Theodorus replied, "At first it was almost unbearable, and I wished for death as a speedy release. But just when I was about to expire from the pain, I saw beside me a young man who wiped the bloody sweat from my body with a soft, cool handkerchief. He said to me, 'Be of good cheer; the Lord is with you.' From that moment until my torturers gave up," Theodorus continued, "I was free from pain and fear. When I was untied from the rack, the young man quietly disappeared."

Only Theodorus saw the angel, and the comfort he received from that heavenly visitor sustained him to meet every further trial that awaited him in his long life of witnessing for Jesus.

❧ ❧ ❧ ❧

In all of history, no account of angelic support matches the poignancy of Christ's experience in Gethsemane. In that secluded garden at the foot of Mount Olivet, Jesus agonized over the price He must pay to ransom and redeem the human race. All heaven watched in suspense to see what decision He would make in the face of Satan's supernaturally skillful tactics. Is it any wonder that He prayed, "Oh, My Father, if it be possible let this cup pass from Me"?

In the extremity of His anguish and spiritual separation from the Father, the Just suffering for the unjust, Jesus sweat great drops of blood and came close to dying from the crushing weight of supernatural grief. Then something marvelous happened in that Garden where our Lord groaned and pleaded with God for some alternative way, that He knew in His heart could not be. The Father sent an angel to help Christ drink the cup of suffering and judgment on our behalf, that He might be able to offer with nail-pierced hands the cup of salvation and joy to us.

With inspired insight, the author of *The Desire of Ages* described this crucial juncture of Christ's ordeal: "Angels had longed to bring relief to the divine sufferer, but this might not be. No way of escape was found for the Son of God. In this awful crisis, when everything was at stake, when the mysterious cup trembled in the hand of the sufferer, the heavens opened, a light shone forth amid the stormy darkness of the crisis hour, and the mighty angel who stands in God's presence, occupying the position from which Satan fell, came to the side of Christ. The angel came not to take the cup from Christ's hand, but to strengthen Him to drink it, with the assurance of the Father's love. He came to give power to the divine-human suppliant. He pointed Him to the open heavens, telling Him of the souls that would be saved as the result of His sufferings. He assured Him that His Father is greater and more powerful than Satan, that His death would result in the utter discomfiture of Satan, and that the kingdom of this world would be given to the saints of the Most High. He told Him that He would see the travail of His soul and be satisfied, for He would see a multitude of the human race saved, eternally saved" (*The Desire of Ages*, pp. 693, 694).

❦ ❦ ❦ ❦

Christ wishes to give those who trust Him "full assurance of faith," the very blessing that Satan most dreads our having. Josephine B. of Williamsport, Maryland tells the story of the special work of angels in bringing comfort to her mother at a crucial period in her life.

"My 98-year-old mother, Hilah, was almost blind, and had life-threatening health problems, when she discovered that she was afraid of dying. This seemed strange to us, considering her faithful, life-long commitment to God. Yet I have discovered that many Christians are shaky about the assurance of salvation.

"I talked and prayed with my mother, and read Bible verses to her about trust in God, such as Psalm 56:3, 4: 'When I am afraid, I will trust in you. In God, whose word I praise, in God I trust; I will not be afraid' (NIV). One evening Mother had a spell during which it seemed that her heart almost stopped. We were greatly relieved to see this episode pass, as her heartbeat returned to normal. I didn't know what her feelings were, but the next morning when she awoke, she asked excitedly, 'Did you see all the angels?'

"I looked at her a little puzzled, and she continued, 'Oh, my, all those angels I saw!' Then as she realized that my dad and I had not seen what she had seen, she said to us, 'I wish you could have seen them! They all looked as though they were coming down to welcome me.'

"She related with joy that during the previous night she had been in the backyard (which was surely a fantasy or a dream, for she had not been outside the house), and all of a sudden the sky was full of angels! She described how the angels were circling around, filling the sky with their beauty and brightness. Then they came very near to her, and she felt their power. She supposed that they had come to take her away, but they did not. After a while they went back into heaven.

" 'It's going to be grand!' she exclaimed, thinking of the time when the angels actually will come with Jesus to take the redeemed to be with Him. She sang a snatch of the song, 'We'll

Never Say Good-bye in Heaven,' which I hadn't heard for years. A little later she sang, in her very elderly voice, 'Jesus Is the Sweetest Name I Know.'

"Hilah loved to relate this experience of seeing the angels. I think that God gave her a vision of angels to let her know how much He loved her and that she had nothing to fear. She continued to be highly motivated to live, and passed her 100th birthday, but she never again gave any indication that she feared death!"

❦ ❦ ❦ ❦

Jesus has promised never to leave us nor forsake us (see Isaiah 43:1-6). This promise is sure, and we certainly do need its support in these times of difficulty and danger.

John F., a pastor, was traveling alone from Wyoming to his new pastorate in New Jersey. This journey was the most sorrowful of all his life. His beloved wife had gone spiritually adrift and ended their marriage in order to take up with a same-sex companion. Fifteen years of marriage and service together had turned to dust. Never had life seemed so desolate and lonely. Pastor John had to assume residence and work in a completely new area—away from the pain and loss, away from the consternation of grieving church members who felt as helpless in the face of this tragedy as he did.

Knowing the journey was long, Pastor John wanted to cover as many miles as he could each day. He prayed that God would be by his side all the way and send an angel to keep his misting eyes from blinding him with tears. He prayed for comfort, and it came. From time to time as he crossed the vast expanse of his beloved Wyoming he felt the sustaining presence of a divine being with him. He was able to look forward to the future with some hope.

As John came toward the eastern end of Wyoming he felt very tired. He saw a sign indicating that a motel and diner lay 17 miles ahead in Bushnell, Nebraska. *That's where I'll stop,* John decided. *I'll spend the night. If only I can hold out until then, I'm so tired,* he thought. *Oh, Lord, be with me,* he prayed.

Moments later John fell asleep at the wheel.

The next thing he knew, a voice called to him, "Wake up, John." Arousing, he looked ahead and saw himself cruising along the road at the allowed speed. His hands were firmly on the wheel. Immediately to the right a sign appeared that read, "Bushnell Exit 1/2 mile." By now John was really awake. It struck him: *I've been sleeping for the past 15 miles or so. Thank You Lord for preserving my life.*

Pulling off at the exit, John went to the nearest gas station. Two attendants were sitting outside, smoking and chatting on this summer's night. Ambling over to the car a few moments later, one filled the tank while the other washed the car windows. Learning from the attendant where the nearest motel was, John paid him and said good night.

"Just a minute, sir," the attendant said, concern written on his face. "Where's the other feller that was with you? Did he go to the rest room? You don't want to leave him behind, do you?"

"What fellow?" John asked.

"You know, that young blond guy that was sitting next to you in the passenger's seat. My partner and I both saw him as you drove in."

John knew that the attendant had seen his angel, while he himself was only dimly and sporadically aware of his presence. But how could he explain this to the puzzled attendant? "Oh, he's my traveling companion. Sometimes you can see him, and sometimes he's invisible."

"Oh, I see. Sure, mister, sure. You have a good night now," said the attendant, uneasily backing away.

❦ ❦ ❦

Angels bring us comfort and protection on the highway, in the home, and even in the house of the Lord, as Carla W. of Ooltewah, Tennessee has discovered. After reading Tim Crosby and Lonnie Melashenko's book *In The Presence of Angels,* Carla sent in this account of her own experience:

"I want to share with you the help and encouragement God

and my angel have given me in my life. Remembering these experiences encourages me in down times and helps me look above this world and all its pain.

"When I was 6 I fell down a flight of steps to our basement. My mother came running. I remember telling her, 'I'm fine, my angel held my head.' I well remember having felt the support of his hands.

"At 12 I was riding my bike along a very busy intersection of Takoma Park, Maryland, when my handlebar hit a signpost and threw me out into the busy intersection. I heard the squealing of brakes and closed my eyes. When I opened them, my head and body were under a car, the wheel not two inches from my head.

"Since age 9, I had problems with seeing my dead grandmother and other relatives. I did not realize that these apparitions could not have been my dead relatives. Fortunately, I attended a Seventh-day Adventist school, J. N. Andrews, and confided the problem to my third-grade teacher, Mary R. She explained these experiences to me from the Bible and told me I could ask aloud for Jesus to be with me whenever one of these apparitions appeared. That's what I did.

"Several of my relatives are spiritualists, and they told me when I was 9 that the spirits informed them I was to be a special medium. I replied that their activities were of the devil and that I would have no part of it. However, they kept after me for a long time.

"While I held onto my faith in my teen years, I later lost my way through an ill-advised marriage. I became bitter and resentful over my lot. Finally this painful relationship ended, and two years later my life changed completely. I was in New York visiting an elderly Christian aunt. Hesitantly I attended church with her on Sabbath. The pastor gave a beautiful sermon on God's great love and forgiveness for each of us. But even while listening to this message of hope, accusing thoughts crowded into my mind. I kept hearing a raspy voice saying, 'Forget it, it's too late for you.'

"As we all rose to sing for the altar call, a rich warmth came over me. Then a voice distinctly spoke to me, 'Carla, go forth, you've hesitated too long. Go forth, Carla.' Instantly I had a wonderful sense of freedom and went forward. Soon after that, Elder Robert Z. rebaptized me at my home church. No one really knew I had left God, so no doubt some were surprised to see me being rebaptized.

"My heart burst with joy as I went down into the water. I felt the value of Christ's sacrifice for me as never before. I knew that He loved me all along but would never force my will.

"As I was changing in the church dressing room, I suddenly became very fearful. I began to be tortured by the thought that I had fooled myself and wasn't really forgiven and accepted by God. My joy quickly changed to deep depression and discouragement. As I made my way back into the sanctuary, a deacon I had known since my childhood saw me but didn't speak to me. I became ashamed and felt sure that I had deceived myself and that my sins were still upon me. I told no one of my feelings. In the sanctuary, all during the church service I prayed and prayed, telling God all my fears.

"Afterward family and friends came up to me. I smiled and hid my true feelings. Suddenly a little old lady pushed her way through all the people to come directly up to me. She stood very close to me and grasped my hand tightly. I was taken with her bright youthful eyes that looked like the heavens behind her glasses. Looking at me very meaningfully she said, "Don't worry honey, you are whiter than white." She turned to leave. I wanted to ask her how she knew, but she had disappeared. I was overwhelmed afresh with joy and had no doubt that I had met my angel. Then I thanked God for accepting Jesus' sacrifice for me.

"Since that time my life has been filled with comfort and the joy of believing."

❧ ❧ ❧ ❧

George Matheson (1842-1906) began to lose his sight before he was a year old. By the time he was 17 he was almost completely blind. But despite this handicap George attended the University of Glasgow, where he gained his bachelor's and master's degrees with distinction. This was before the days when special schools and facilities for the blind were available in Britain.

George deeply loved a very refined and spiritual young lady who for a time reciprocated his affections. They became engaged to marry, but she could not rise above the thought of her fiancé's blindness. Tearfully she broke off the engagement, leaving George a broken-hearted, lonely young man. Never again did he attempt to gain the affections of a woman. For him marriage was a closed question, not because of bitterness or self-pity, but because he did not wish to put any young woman through the test of dealing with his affliction.

At the age of 26 George was appointed as parish minister at Innellan on the Firth of Clyde, a beautiful, idyllic setting. There he had a long and fruitful ministry. Yet pain and loneliness proved to be his lot in life. Undoubtedly, he thought from time to time of what life would have been like had his betrothed accepted his blindness and joined her life with his. In his private hours at the parsonage of Innellan, George took refuge in writing. He was a prolific poet and writer of devotional articles and books.

In his thirties another test awaited George, which in many respects pierced his heart more keenly than his fiancée's withdrawn affections in earlier days. His church began to drift into theological liberalism as a result of embracing the theories of Darwin. Every fiber of George's being was bound up with the spiritual welfare and safety of God's people, and as he saw his efforts to uphold truth and combat error receive little appreciation, he felt terribly isolated. George agonized over the crisis as only a deeply spiritual man could.

One day while he contemplated these troubles and contended with a deep sense of personal rejection and loss in the midst of it all, a new hymn came to George's mind. He wrote it down in just a few minutes and never felt any burden to retouch it, because he believed that it had come to him as a gift from the Lord. Though a prolific writer, never had any composition come to him so easily as this. And never did he write anything more beautiful. It is a profound statement of faith and devotion. George felt that this poem had been dictated to him by an inner voice.

We think that inner voice was from an angel, who gave this poem not only to sustain George's faith, but also the faith of countless believers in all future days until that golden hour when faith becomes sight. Isaiah records, "You shall have a song as in the night as when a holy festival is kept, and gladness of heart as when one goes with a flute, to come into the mountain of the Lord, to the Mighty One of Israel" (Isaiah 30:29). And who is better able to teach us these songs in the night than the angels of heaven, who constantly sing praises to God's name, and are always encompassed with the beauty of His holiness?

Here is the poem, which is included in many hymnals of all denominations:

*O Love that will not let me go; I rest my weary soul in Thee;*
*I give Thee back the life I owe, that in Thy ocean depths its flow*
*May richer, fuller be.*

*O Light that followest all my way, I yield my flickering torch to Thee;*
*My heart restores its borrowed ray, that in Thy sunshine's blaze its day*
*May brighter, fairer be.*

*O Joy that seekest me through pain, I cannot close my heart to Thee;*
*I trace the rainbow through the rain, and feel the promise is not vain*
*That morn shall tearless be.*

*O Cross that liftest up my head, I dare not ask to fly from Thee;*
*I lay in dust life's glory dead, and from the ground there blossoms red*
*Life that shall endless be.*
—George Matheson, 1882.

---

1. Adapted from *Susan Haskell: Missionary*, by Ivy R. Doherty (Review and Herald, 1958), pp. 20-27.

# CHAPTER THREE

# *Evil Angels*

Three men in military dress groped their way over craggy terrain one misty night. Their sinister mission demanded the cover of darkness. Reaching their destination, a remote mountain hut, they rapped on the door with an authority that hid their uneasiness. A bedraggled, bleary woman opened the door a crack and in a raspy voice inquired, "Yes?"

"I want you to call up the ghost of a man whom I shall name."

With a hiss of fear the old woman replied, "Don't you know that Saul has had all the mediums and wizards in the land killed? Are you trying to trap me so that I'll die?"

"As surely as God lives, I promise that you shall not die."

Warily, the sorceress allowed her unwanted visitors to enter her dingy parlor, where her smoking lamp yielded a lean flame.

"Whom shall I bring up to you?" she quavered in an eerie voice.

"Samuel."

After practicing her incantations, the medium saw a shape emerge from the misty realms of the spirit world. As the "ghost" of Samuel the prophet took form, the medium shrieked with a realization that her mysterious visitor was King Saul. But quickly calming her fears, Saul entered into conversation with the shadowy figure purporting to be the deceased prophet. This figure predicted Saul's death the next day at the hands of the Philistines.

The grim prediction proved true.

Had Saul, on the last day of his bitter, broken life, really spoken with the spirit or ghost of Samuel? Why did he attempt this esoteric form of communication? Scripture tells us that Saul had so wandered from faith in God that the Lord no longer answered him by dreams, prophets, or oracles. This makes it clear that the source of Saul's information on that fateful night was not divine.

What had gone wrong, so that God would no longer communicate with Saul? Saul had plunged into stubborn rebellion against heaven's way of truth and holiness. He had to have things his way. He obeyed God only when it fit his own plans or inclination. This is not obedience at all. The prophet Samuel, before he died, had rebuked Saul for his open disregard of God's express commands:

"Hath the Lord as great delight in burnt offerings and sacrifices, as in obeying the voice of the Lord? Behold, to obey is better than sacrifice, and to hearken than the fat of rams. For rebellion is as the sin of witchcraft, and stubbornness is as iniquity and idolatry. Because thou hast rejected the word of the Lord, he hath also rejected thee from being king" (1 Samuel 15:22, 23, KJV).

Having rejected God, Saul now turned to a source of information God had strictly forbidden people to dabble with—communication with the supposed spirits of the dead. Through the writings of Moses God had expressed this prohibition.

" 'There shall not be found among you anyone who makes his son or his daughter pass through the fire, or one who practices witchcraft, or a soothsayer, or one who interprets omens, or a sorcerer, or one who conjures spells, or a medium, or spiritist, or one who calls up the dead. For all who do these things are an abomination to the Lord' " (Deuteronomy 18:10-12).

This is strong language. It is a warning of love, because the whole realm of occult arts is under the direct control of Satan. God forbids communication with the dead, because it can't really be done (see Ecclesiastes 9:5, 6, 10; Psalm 115:17; Psalm 146:4). The righteous dead sleep in Jesus until His Second Coming (see Job 14:12-14; 1 Corinthians 15:22; 1 Thessalonians 4:16, 17).

So to whom was Saul speaking? The being looked and sounded like Samuel. It spoke with the same kind of prophetic authority that Samuel possessed in his life. Yet it wasn't Samuel, but a demonic impersonator. 1 Chronicles 10:13 says that the "Samuel" with whom Saul spoke at that seance was a "familiar spirit." The dictionary defines a "familiar spirit" as a demon or evil spirit.

In our time communication with "the dead" is a common occurrence. Its popularity has risen through Hollywood movies that portray spiritualism as a delightful, entertaining, and generally harmless thing. Referring to a recent occult movie, *Los Angeles Times* correspondent Marshall Fine wrote, "With 'What Dreams May Come,' all approaches to the post-living experience are honored, in a film that blends every idea about the afterlife into one creamy metaphysical slush. . . . The basic idea here is that we create our own paradises out of what's in our heads" (Oct. 2, 1998).

This review pointedly states Satan's underlying strategy in the occult. His objective is to make everything look ultimately acceptable in an "anything goes" universe. No moral absolutes, no divine rule, no cosmic plan, just an endless journey into the unknown whose meaning you develop for yourself as you go along. Philosophers call this solipsism. *It is nothing less than self-generated delusion with background assistance from Satan.* (See also Jeremiah 10:23; 1 Timothy 4:1.)

This nebulous program is far different from God's sure word of promise: "For I know the thoughts that I think toward you, says the Lord, thoughts of peace and not of evil, to give you a future and a hope. Then you will call upon Me and go and pray to Me, and I will listen to you. And you will seek Me and find Me, when you search for Me with all your heart" (Jeremiah 29:11-13).

❧ ❧ ❧ ❧

Evangelist Roy Allan Anderson tells the story of one of his encounters with the spirit world.

" 'I'm through with God!' he shouted as I stepped into his office. 'I don't want you here. In fact, I don't want to see you again ever. I'm through.'

"Strange words from a friend, especially when we had been so close. I had always been welcomed into his office, but not that morning. What had gone wrong? What had changed his attitude?

"I soon discovered the reason. He had just returned from a spiritualistic seance, the first he had attended for many years. To him it was unfortunate that I arrived just at that moment. He was still reveling in the aftereffects of his conversation with an important apparition, a Pharaoh of ancient Egypt.

"The atmosphere was tense. This was a showdown, and we both knew it. The first time I met this city official and his family was at a large evangelistic meeting. I was in New Zealand at that time, and at that meeting I had spoken on 'The Bible as the Word of God.' This man and his wife and three daughters made themselves known to me and invited me to visit them at their hilltop home. I was happy to go. They were very friendly, and before long they looked upon me as 'one of the family.'

"Not only the father and the mother but also the three girls studied the Bible eagerly with me. From the very first, however, I noticed something unusual about that father; he never seemed completely at ease when we touched the question of death and the resurrection. Later I learned that he had been a member of an important spiritualistic circle and for years had practiced clairvoyance, even serving as a medium. But that was twenty-five years before. Since then, he had never attended a spiritualistic meeting or a seance.

"He was an important figure in that city. He had never been a

Christian, and when I met him, he seemed to be entirely irreligious. When I got closer to him, I learned that he had a constant companion, a 'familiar spirit,' as the Bible terms it in Leviticus 19:31. It claimed to be a female spirit, and while not visible to anyone else, that power was there continually, I later learned. She called herself Nancy and was as real to him as any member of his family. She was tall, with long, flowing tresses.

"He rarely made a decision without consulting that spirit, and remarkably, he got his answers. If he needed a direct Yes or No, he would quietly appeal to this spirit entity, and his hand would be lifted six or eight inches from the desk. The number of thumps would indicate the decision. When once that power took control, neither he nor anyone else could hold that arm still. He was no weakling; on the contrary, he stood about six feet four in height. He was well built and weighed 225 pounds. In his younger days he had been a champion heavyweight boxer. Apart from those rather simple responses from Nancy, spiritualism apparently played no part in his life.

"During those twenty-five years he encountered no problem with the spirits, but when he began to study the Bible, things changed rapidly. Of course, he was well acquainted with unseen powers; but he came to know that such powers are not all from God. Some are definitely evil. Learning what the Bible says on this subject, he decided to have nothing more to do with spirits.

"Having made his decision, he began to encounter real opposition. The first came from the spirit Nancy. When she failed to turn him against the Bible, a whole group of spirits united to withstand him. Still he and his family continued to study the Word of God. Sometimes we studied together late into the night.

"Before long the spirits began to oppose me personally, first by argument, then by physical force. One night as we finished our study of the twelfth chapter of Revelation, the spirits said to him, 'What you have been discussing here tonight is all wrong. We have the key to the whole situation, and we give you this as the symbol.' With those words a large key, nearly eight inches long, fell to the floor from apparently nowhere. All were startled. Then one of the girls reached over and picked it up. No one had ever seen it before.

"On another occasion, an apparition appeared in the form of the family's pet dog, a champion fox terrier, that had recently died. For years the man had bred champions. And when that sharp-nosed little creature jumped up on his lap in the accustomed way, the family was, of course, deeply impressed. But by that time they all knew something of the deceptive power of the spirit world. What seemed almost overwhelming evidence of survival after death, they knew was just another effort by evil spirits to deceive.

"Many strange things happened during the next few months, for the battle was growing more intense. Sometimes as I left that home the spirits would say, 'We will get rid of Anderson tonight on his way home.' And they often tried! More than once I have felt the stranglehold of unseen hands clutching my throat and forcing me to the ground. There is no question in one's mind concerning the existence of invisible powers when he is faced with such experiences as these.

"I knew I was wrestling 'not against flesh and blood,' as the apostle Paul said, but 'against wicked spirits in high places' (Ephesians 6:12). How wicked these spirits really are I came to realize when, for example, that father, moved by one of them, grasped his seventeen-year-old daughter by the throat and with fingers of steel began choking her to death. Usually he was the embodiment of kindness. But on this occasion he flew into a rage because she had said the Bible was indeed the Word of God and the only safe guide. Sensing her danger, I stepped forward and in the name of Jesus Christ commanded him to release her. His grip relaxed immediately.

"For months I studied the Bible with that New Zealand family. In fact, I lived with the family for three months while my wife and little son were visiting loved ones in Australia. It gave me an eerie feeling to hear, as I did many times, that father pass my door in the middle of the night and go down the stairway to the living room. I knew why he was going. It was to hold a private seance. And when he got there, the piano would usually start playing of its own accord. He was no musician; he did not know one note from another, but the piano played by itself. It was always the same song, about Polly who died and was now looking down from heaven.

"The months I spent as a guest in that home were pleasurable in most ways, but also a real strain. To battle with evil powers for the soul of a man, and sense the struggle becoming more intense with every passing week, is something one would not willingly choose. We worshiped together each day, and it was a joy to see those dear folk taking hold of God's Word.

"After my wife and little son returned from Australia and we were back in our own home again, I was awakened one morning about five o'clock by a voice that spoke as clearly and distinctly as any I have ever heard. The words were those of our Lord Himself: 'This kind goeth not out but by prayer and fasting.'

"At once I recognized this as a call from God. I awakened my wife, and we prayed earnestly. We both were convinced that God wanted me to visit this man in his office. His work in that city was akin to that of a magistrate and was particularly concerned with pensions. He was a well-respected citizen, and his office was in the heart of the business section.

"Before going to see him, I stopped at the office of a doctor friend, in whose prayers I had occasion to have real confidence. We had prayed through many situations before. So, while his patients waited, I related to him the happenings of that morning. Together we sought God's help for whatever lay ahead.

"When I arrived at this man's office, so familiar to me, he blurted out: 'Anderson, what are you doing here? I don't want to see you again—ever!' He had a look of hatred in his eyes. As already mentioned, he was a massively built man, and as a police officer and a detective he had been trained to brook no argument from anyone. Now he was demon-possessed, and he looked it!

" 'I'm through with God,' he shouted.

" 'But God is not through with you,' I replied.

" 'Why should I bother with God? I have the highest honor that can ever come to a man,' he said.

" 'What is that?' I asked.

" 'I have the "White Wings of Egypt," ' he said with a sneer. 'And no harm can ever come to me. The spirits have assured me that I can go anywhere, and my life is perfectly safe.'

"Then with a fiendish chuckle he told how he had gone to a spirit medium early that morning. He related how he had commanded the medium to bring up for him one of the ancient Pharaohs, calling him by name. The medium became alarmed and begged to be excused, for she said, 'You evidently belong to a higher circle of spirits from those I know, and the one you are calling is very high. Please, don't use me—go to someone else.'

"For the moment he became the old police officer, and demanded obedience. She was soon in a trance. When the Pharaoh apparition appeared, he claimed to have a special message for him. 'You must stop studying the Bible,' the Pharaoh ordered. 'I have greater truth than that old obsolete book.'

"During that seance this man also communed with another spirit purporting to be his first wife, who had died more than twenty years earlier. To prove her identity this apparition rubbed a handkerchief across his hands, laden with perfume—the same perfume he had given his bride on the night of their wedding. And I can testify that when I met him a few minutes later his hands exuded perfume in such quantity that the office was filled with the odor. Of course, some doubter will say he had the perfume in his office all the time. But none who have had experience with unseen powers will find cause for doubt.

"When that spirit interview came to a close, the Pharaoh conferred on him the covering of the 'White Wings of Egypt,' saying, 'This is a special honor, the highest honor we can ever give to a human being, and it comes to you with the blessing of all ancient Egypt.'

"When that man came back to his office, he was elated. His

whole countenance was changed. Just then I arrived and walked straight in, as usual.

"But things were not as usual. He was belligerent and wanted nothing to do with me or with God. Here was a desperate situation, and it presented a real challenge. There sat my friend, the one in whose home I had spent months in happy fellowship as we studied the Word of God together. Now he was far from God, blaspheming His name, and defiantly ordering me out of his office. Repeatedly he shouted, 'I'm through with God.'

"What could I do? Should I leave as he had ordered me, or should I defy the spirits? I moved closer to him and, putting my hand on his shoulder, took an old Bible from the shelf in his office. It was the one he used when individuals were required to give information under oath.

"I moved slowly, for I was lifting my heart silently to God in prayer. I fingered the pages for a moment, and then, in a strange way that Bible seemed to open naturally at the thirtieth chapter of Isaiah. I began to read aloud:

'Woe to the rebellious children, says the Lord, who take counsel, but not of Me, and who devise plans, but not of My Spirit, that they may add sin to sin; who walk to go down to Egypt, and have not asked at My advice, to strengthen themselves in the strength of Pharaoh, and to trust in the shadow of Egypt! Therefore the strength of Pharaoh shall be your shame, and the trust in the shadow of Egypt shall be your humiliation' (Isaiah 30:1-3).

"He jumped up, grabbed the Bible out of my hand, and shouted, 'That's not there—you're making it up!'

" 'It *is* there,' I replied. 'Read it yourself.'

"He took the Bible in his trembling hands and reread those verses aloud. Then he slumped back into his chair as if struck.

"Kindly but firmly I said, 'Dad,' (for that's what I called him) 'the road you have taken is the road to confusion and ultimate destruction, and you know it. You are putting your trust in the "shadow of Egypt." You are boasting of a covering, the "White Wings of Egypt." You know this is not of God's Spirit; it is the spirit of the devil. In doing this you are adding sin to sin.'

"He was silent. While he looked wistfully into my face, I read these words in the next chapter. ' "Woe to those that go down to Egypt for help, . . . but who do not look to the Holy One of Israel, Nor seek the Lord!" ' (Isaiah 31:1).

"He looked very solemn. He stepped from his desk and walked over to the door, locking it so that we would not be interrupted. Then, looking into my eyes, he said: 'What shall I do?'

"I said: 'Let us pray to God for forgiveness and deliverance.'

"We did. We offered up earnest prayers that day in his office, and I saw that man claim the victory. It was marvelous to witness his turning from darkness to light. But I was confident the great deceiver would not give up without a struggle. During the next few days some of us who were close friends of this man fasted and prayed that full deliverance might come to him.

"Some weeks later, following a wonderful day of worship, I felt impressed to go and see this man, for he had absented himself from church that day. I took a friend with me, a courageous man who had been decorated for gallantry as an airman in the war. Before going up to the house we prayed, and then I phoned to say we were coming. The wife met us at the door and led us into the living room.

"As soon as I entered, I sensed that things were anything but reassuring, for there sat our friend in silent communion with the spirits. I had seen him on other occasions sitting on the davenport talking to his spirit friend, Nancy. He spoke no words. It was thought communion.

"We waited a few minutes; then, beginning our conversation in a casual strain at first, I tried to open up the question we wanted to discuss with him. That very day the church had decided to ask his wife to serve as a deaconess. As soon as I mentioned that, his attitude changed. He became adamant, and for an hour and a half he opposed everything we suggested.

"Seeing we were getting nowhere, I rose to leave. In doing so, however, I said, 'I have never left this home without having prayer, and I do not intend to tonight. Let us kneel together.'

"This took him somewhat off guard. Naturally he was in no mood to pray, but out of respect he cooperated. He had the same leering smirk that I had seen at other times when he had been communing with spirits. In our family worships, this man always knelt at a certain place in that room, using the piano stool for support. I suggested that he do so again. He did, but reluctantly.

"Then I asked the friend I had brought along to pray. Scarcely had he begun when I sensed something was wrong. My friend seemed hardly able to speak. I knew what it was, for I, myself, was passing through the same experience. We were being 'pressured' by an unseen power. It is a harrowing experience to feel every inch of one's body under pressure, which becomes stronger every moment. We could scarcely breathe, much less speak.

"Then the door opened of its own accord, and in came a huge apparition, appearing as a knight in shining armor and holding aloft an upturned Turkish scimitar. At the sight, my friend, this powerfully built former police officer and leader of a detective squad, sprang from his place. Throwing one arm around his wife's neck and the other around mine, he clung to us, trembling like a frightened child!

"The situation was desperate, for this spirit threatened to kill him. Summoning all the strength I could, I challenged, 'In the name of Jesus Christ, I command the devils to leave this house at once.'

"What followed was terrific! Never before or since have I heard anything like it. Hell seemed to be let loose! Windows rattled, doors slammed, and the whole house shook as if by an earthquake. We heard shrieking and yelling. The house rocked, but we remained on our knees until at last the uproar ceased. The calm that followed was as impressive as the tumult before.

"As we rose from our knees, we looked at each other in amazement. That man's look of terror was gone, but he was still shaking. Now he knew that God was there, in the very place that had been rattled by the powers of hell. He also knew that the power of Jesus Christ is far greater than that of Satan.

"To call upon the name of Jesus for protection and then feel the vise-like grip of the enemy relax is tremendous. More than a year passed, however, before my friend was really free. I know that spiritualists will say that those opposing powers were 'bad spirits,' but that the 'good spirits' can be trusted, for they protect and never harm. That is exactly what this man himself believed when first we met. For remember that he, too, had been a leading spiritualist. But he soon discovered, as thousands of others have, that even the so-called 'good spirits' of the occult are deceivers. They will use their powers against the very ones who once paid them homage."[1]

❧ ❧ ❧ ❧

In its early years, revived spiritualism openly declared its hostility to the Bible and to the belief in Jesus Christ as the Savior of humanity. Spiritualism boasted of its intention to supplant Christianity and make it obsolete. But in recent years Satan has shifted his strategy. He has reserved his greatest deceptions for these last days of Earth's history.

Will Baron, in his fascinating book, *Deceived by the New Age*, tells the story of Satan's "converted" tactics. In 1980 Baron became a member of a New Age cult called the Lighted Way, founded in the 1960s by a psychic medium whom he calls Muriel. As a channeler, she came under the instruction of Djawhl Khul, a purported guru from the spirit world. Djawhl Khul claimed to have been a Tibetan priest who served as the abbot of a Lamasery several centuries before. His spoken messages through Muriel were about love, brotherhood, and consciousness elevation. They included teachings on reincarnation, astrology, numerology, metaphysical writings, tarot cards, and psychic readings.

It was through Muriel's startlingly accurate psychic reading of him that Will Baron was drawn into her movement, which she claimed was not a religion but a spiritual fellowship. By connecting with this movement, Baron entered into some profoundly mystical experiences and became a channeler himself.

After four years of involvement with the Lighted Way, Baron was astounded to learn through a message given to Muriel that it was now time for the followers to discard all their occult books and turn exclusively to the worship of Jesus, using the Bible as their sole textbook. On the surface this sounds wonderful.

But the Jesus who channeled through Muriel was anything but the Jesus of Scripture. It was a system of self-elevation reached by cultivating the Christ consciousness within. True, a being named Jesus Christ appeared in visions and channeling sessions, but the teachings were widely at variance with Bible truth. For instance, the Second Coming was presented as no more than a personal spiritual experience, a redeeming encounter with Christ. Immortality was defined as a blessing "achieved" through meditational states that modulate the participant more and more into the image of the divine. Christ as an atoning sacrifice for sin, Christ as the Creator of the Universe, was not recognized. He was simply an ascended Master in a brotherhood of Masters.

Baron was driven by his channeled "Christ" into preaching this spiritualistic gospel at the mall and on the beach. His guiding voice became more and more demanding, dictatorial, and unreasonable, forcing him into heavy debt in order to give donations to the Lighted Way. Despite numerous "healings" through his mentor Muriel, his health steadily declined. The healings were of short duration, but the aftermath of weakness and nervous instability increased.

Eventually, Baron violently reacted against this dictatorial inner voice calling itself Jesus. He cursed this entity in a fit of uncontrolled rage. Then he repented and submitted once again to its control. Commenting on his journey as a devotee of the Lighted Way movement, Baron writes:

"You may be wondering if I ever had any doubts regarding the identity of the spirit that ruled my life—whether he was the true Jesus. The truth is I never suspected I was a slave to demons masquerading as agents of light. My confidence in the New Age path and the spirit guides had built up over many years. Once I had read the Alice Bailey books, I became a devoted believer in the New Age, its spirit guides, and its philosophies. I then became an easy candidate for total 'possession.' Almost nothing could shake my faith in what I believed and cause me to doubt the authenticity of my spirit guide. Even my dedicated Bible reading could not pierce through the web of deception because I was twisting the meaning of many texts in an attempt to harmonize them with my existing metaphysical beliefs."[2]

Despite his belief in the Bible and in Jesus, Baron was deceived by a twisted interpretation of the Scripture. Paul wrote about this danger—the danger of a demonically controlled interpretation of God's Word itself. He wrote, "But I fear, lest somehow, as the serpent deceived Eve by his craftiness, so your minds may be corrupted from the simplicity that is in Christ. For if he who comes preaches another Jesus whom we have not preached, or if you receive a different spirit which you have not received, or a different gospel which you have not accepted—you may well put up with it!" (2 Corinthians 11:3, 4, NKJV). False Christs, false gospels, false prophets—their proliferation demands that we know the truth about Jesus as it is presented in God's Word, correctly interpreted, letting the Scriptures be their own expositor, rather than believing some strange spirit or guru.

---

1. From Roy Allen Anderson, *Secrets of the Spirit World* (Pacific Press, 1966), pp. 1-9.

2. Will Baron, *Deceived By the New Age* (Pacific Press, 1990), p. 157.

# CHAPTER FOUR

# Angel Evangelists

Without doubt, the primary work of angels is to cooperate with God for the salvation of people. The world's salvation is the Lord's highest priority. Scripture declares that angels are "ministering spirits sent forth to minister for those who will inherit salvation" (Hebrews 1:14).

For these brilliant heaven-sent messengers, the plan of redemption is one of all-absorbing interest. Peter expressed it thus: "Concerning this salvation, the prophets, who spoke of the grace that was to come to you, searched intently and with the greatest care, trying to find out the time and circumstances to which the Spirit of Christ in them was pointing. . . . *Even angels long to look into these things*" (1 Peter 1:10-12, NIV, emphasis supplied).

The angels' fascination and involvement with our salvation is demonstrated by their intense activity in the heavenly sanctuary. The book of Revelation frequently mentions their presence as ministering agents with Jesus in His sanctuary. He sends them out to bring conviction, guidance, dreams, and messages to His people.

Santiago, a literature evangelist in Peru, was visiting homes in an area where the local religious leaders strongly opposed the distribution of Bible literature. These leaders succeeded quite well in arousing hostility to Santiago's work in a certain town where most of the men were employed in one large factory. The plant manager was especially hostile to representatives of "outside" religions. This was not an easily penetrated environment.

But Santiago had a deep burden on his heart to take the message of salvation to this town. For several weeks he made it a matter of intensive prayer, and finally was impressed to select May 15 of that year as the day he would go to the factory and ask the manager for about twenty minutes with all the workers together on the shop floor.

Determined that no opponent should discover his purpose, Santiago prayed in silence and planned in secrecy. He told no one—not his wife, not his district leader, not the church; and he made no written notes concerning his plan. He and God alone knew his intentions for May 15. In his mind he set 9:00 A.M. as the hour for this momentous visit. The only clue was that several weeks beforehand, Santiago (without explanation) placed a very large order for books in optimistic anticipation of the outcome.

Santiago fasted and prayed on May 14 and also the next morning. After lingering at home for a few extra minutes of prayer, he went out with courage and anxiety mingled in his heart. Coming to the closely guarded factory gate at 9:10 A.M., he gave his name to the armed guard, who smiled and said, "Come in, come in; you're late. Mr. Rosado, the manager, is expecting you."

Astonished and grateful for the providence of being mistaken for another, Santiago briskly followed a second guard, who conducted him through a series of corridors and doors directly to Mr. Rosado's office. "Ah, there you are," boomed Mr. Rosado, "I've been expecting you! Come in. You are fifteen minutes late."

Santiago, now puzzled, said, "Pardon me, Mr. Rosado, could it be that you are expecting someone else?"

Shooting a quick look at him, the manager asked, "You are Santiago, the man who has come to show me some books?"

"Yes," he replied with mounting amazement.

"Well, your agent visited with me yesterday and told me you would be here. He has already explained the nature of your mission and material. He has showed me the kind of books that you have to sell and described their educational benefits. Then he said that you planned to be here at nine o'clock today. So I have asked all our workers to assemble on the main shop floor. They're waiting downstairs for you now, so let's go. Time is precious in your business and mine."

Walking as if in a dream, Santiago followed the manager onto the shop floor. Several hundred expectant men stood watching. Praying for guidance, Santiago began to speak in a clear, full voice and gave his canvass in about ten minutes. When he ended, the manager stood up and said, "Men, everything that he is telling you is true. You should buy these books because they will help you and your families have sober, productive, healthy lives with God's special blessing. Take whatever time you need to place your orders."

Santiago took dozens of orders for books, which he was able to promptly fill because of his previous planning. As he left the factory to head home, he knew beyond question that his "agent" could only have been an angel, paving the way for this humble literature evangelist. For no one else on earth was privy to his plans.

❦ ❦ ❦

A mysterious phone call at midnight awakened Lillian Ngaruiya, a literature evangelist in Nairobi, Kenya. A sweet, melodious voice said, "Please take a copy of *The Triumph of God's Love* to Mr. Kamau on the third floor of the Kencom building. Consider it urgent." Then the phone went dead.

The next day Lillian went to that huge building, only to be told that there was no Mr. Kamau on that floor. When she inquired up and down the building, secretaries all over were asking about the mysterious Mr. Kamau. Finally one of them sent for Lillian and confided to her, "My boss's name is Kamau, but he operates under another name." He was then deputy director of government corporations. Soon Lillian was ushered into his spacious office.

"Mr. Kamau—"

"My name is not Kamau!"

Lillian continued, "Last night I received a phone call asking me to visit your office."

"No, you couldn't have received a phone call about me, for my name is not Kamau. Nobody knows me by that name."

Lillian opened her briefcase and took out *The Triumph of God's Love.* Looking him in the eye, she said kindly, "God knows your name—it is Kamau. It may have been an angel from heaven who called me, but he knows your name."

"There are no such things as angels."

Lillian said, "Mr. Kamau, let me tell you an experience one of my friends had, and you will know that there are angels. This friend does the same work I am doing, except she works in poor homes. One lady said, 'I like the book, but I have only half of the money.' At that moment a stranger knocked on the door and was invited in. He spoke up, 'Go ahead and write the receipt; I will pay the other half of the money.'

"As my friend started to go to another home, this stranger went along with her. She asked him, 'Who are you? What's your name?' He replied, 'That's not important, is it?'

"In the next house, the same thing happened. The lady wanted the book but didn't have enough money. Again the stranger volunteered, 'I will pay the balance.' And then at a third house, the same thing happened. As the two were leaving this house, my friend stopped and demanded, 'Tell me, who *are* you?'

"He asked for a piece of paper," my friend told me, "and wrote something on it.

" 'My name—*Daniel na Siku Zetu (Daniel and Our Day).*

" 'My address—*Sabato ya Kweli (The True Sabbath):*

" 'My village—*Vita Kuu (The Great Controversy).*' (These are the Swahili names of three of the books she was selling.)

"When she looked up, Mr. Kamau, he was gone. She believes and I believe that was an angel."

Mr. Kamau sat in rapt attention. She continued, "Let me tell you another experience. One of our representatives was demonstrating these good books to a friendly family who invited him to stay for dinner. They prepared *two* places for him. After they had washed their hands, they asked, 'Where is your friend?'

" 'My friend? I'm all alone.'

" 'No, we saw someone with you.'

" 'You must have seen my angel,' he replied. 'He works with me.'

"Mr. Kamau, we believe that was an angel in the form of a man."

The director quietly asked, "What do I do now?"

"Buy this wonderful book and study it carefully. You are a wonderful person in the eyes of God."

Mr. Kamau bought the book.[1]

❦ ❦ ❦ ❦

As partners in soul winning, angels do their most effective work when they have human agents through whom to speak and minister. Pastor Neumoel Stima of Sao Paulo, Brazil provided this interesting account of an angel's partnership in helping to win a resistant soul to Christ.

"It was Friday evening. I was finishing a Week of Prayer in a city in southern Brazil. I had preached twice a day at two different locations. Several young people had given their lives to God, but one young man seemed to resist the Holy Spirit. Henrique had come to every meeting with his girlfriend. The couple attended all four meetings every day, hearing the same sermons twice each day. I prayed and worked fervently to draw them to Jesus. But Henrique never responded to the appeals.

"I returned to my room on Thursday night filled with frustration. 'God, what am I doing wrong that I cannot lead this young man to You?' I pleaded. I could not sleep, so I read my Bible and prayed for this young man.

"Henrique had left the evening meeting planning to drive to his parents' home 50 miles away. Halfway to his destination, Henrique's car had a flat tire on the desolate road. He discovered his jack was broken. Fearful, he locked himself into his car and lay down to wait for dawn. He tried to sleep but could not. He kept remembering phrases from the week's sermons: 'God is willing to accept you.' 'Ask God once and He will come.'

"For the first time in his life Henrique prayed. He got out of the car and knelt down on the road. 'God, I don't know how to pray, but if what the pastor said is true, come and help me, please.' He got back into the car.

"Within minutes a car pulled off the road in front of him. A tall, strong man stepped out and offered his help. Henrique told him what had happened. The man changed the tire, then put his enormous hand on Henrique's shoulder and said: 'Young man, I came to tell you that God loves you.' Henrique was startled and asked the man his name, but the man simply said, 'Don't forget, God loves you.' Then he turned toward his car.

"Henrique got into his car, wiped tears from his eyes, then looked up to wave at the man who had helped him. But no one was there. No man, no car. Henrique had not heard a car door slam or an engine start up. He drove home in awed silence.

"Henrique was the first to arrive at the church on Friday evening. He ran to open my car door when I arrived and quickly asked, 'Pastor, can you baptize me?' Startled, I listened to his story.

"The following year I baptized Henrique, and a short time later I performed the wedding ceremony for him and his girlfriend. Today they are faithful members of the church."[2]

❦ ❦ ❦

One of the most creative strategies used by an angel appears in a story that occurred almost exactly one hundred years before Henrique's experience. Arthur S. Maxwell relates the account:

"Many years ago, about 1896 or 1897, a Bible colporteur was walking down Market Street in San Francisco when a stranger stopped him and asked him why he did not take his Bibles and books to a certain valley beyond Sacramento. The colporteur explained that he had never heard of the valley but would be glad to go when he could find the time. Then the stranger bade him good-bye, and disappeared in the crowd.

*That's strange!* the colporteur thought to himself. *I wonder why that man spoke to me. How did he know my business? And why is he interested in that particular valley? I must try to go there some-day.* But the busy days and weeks slipped by, and the colporteur didn't go. Yet somehow he couldn't forget what the stranger had said. Every now and then a voice seemed to say to him, 'Go to that valley.'

"At last he felt he should wait no longer. So he set forth on his journey, taking his Bibles and other books with him. It was a long and tiring trip, for there were no autos in those days. Part of the way he went by train, part on horseback, part on foot. Coming to a wide river, which had not then been bridged, he wondered how he was going to get to the other side. As he waited at the water's edge a man appeared in a rowboat and asked if he wished to cross.

" 'I surely do,' said the colporteur. 'How much will you charge to take me over?'

" 'A dollar,' replied the man, and the colporteur agreed.

"On the way across, the colporteur opened his purse and brought out a silver dollar. It was the only one he had and, having time on his hands, he looked at it with more than usual care. It was a new coin, bright from the mint, but marred by a scratch on the eagle. The date on the coin was 1896. Arriving at the other side, the colporteur gave the boatman the silver dollar and bade him good-bye.

" 'Be sure to call at the first cottage you come to up the valley,' said the boatman as he pulled away.

" 'I will,' said the colporteur, wondering what this might mean and what he would find there.

"Soon he caught sight of a cottage on a hillside about a mile ahead and walked briskly toward it. To his surprise, as he drew near the cottage, the front door opened and three children started running down the hill toward him.

" 'Did you bring our Bible?' they cried. 'Did you bring our Bible?'

" 'Your Bible!' he exclaimed. 'What do you mean? How did you know I have some Bibles?'

" 'Oh,' they cried, 'we've all been praying for a Bible, but Mother didn't have the money to buy one till today. But God sent her the money, so we felt sure He would send us the Bible soon.'

"By this time they were at the house, and the mother was there, all flushed and excited, waiting to tell her story of what had happened. 'It's true,' she said. 'We have wanted a Bible so long. We've been praying for one for many months but somehow could never afford it. Then this afternoon, just after we had all prayed again, a voice seemed to say to me, "Go and look out the front door." So I opened the door and there, lying on the ground, was a silver dollar. It seemed so wonderful that I felt sure God had sent it, and that the Bible would come soon. Sir, does your Bible cost a dollar?'

" 'It does,' he said, 'just a dollar.'

"Opening his case, he took out a Bible and handed it to the mother, who in turn passed over to him the dollar she had found that very afternoon.

"Now it was the colporteur's turn to be astonished. Something about the dollar arrested his attention. It was newly minted but had a scratch on the eagle. And the date was 1896!

" 'Is there something wrong with it?' asked the mother anxiously.

" 'No, no,' he said. 'But, madam, this is the identical dollar I gave to the boatman this very afternoon, less than an hour ago!'

" 'What boatman?' she asked.

" 'At the ferry.'

" 'But there's no ferry; never has been, as long as I've been here.'

" 'But he brought me across the river this very afternoon and told me to come to this cottage; and I gave him this same silver dollar!'

"So they talked on, going over it all again and again, marveling how God works, 'His wonders to perform.'

"The mystery of that silver dollar will perhaps never be solved. But both the colporteur and that godly woman were convinced, as I am, that God was in this thing. He knew of the longing of the dear mother and her children to read His Word; and in His own wonderful way He made it possible for them to receive it.

"And if you wonder about the stranger and boatman, remember that Abraham of old 'entertained angels unawares.' "[3]

❦ ❦ ❦ ❦

Angels serving as partners in soul winning is not a recent development. Their evangelistic activity goes clear back to Bible times. Let's look at one instance in the book of Acts.

"Now *an angel of the Lord* spoke to Philip, saying, 'Arise and go toward the south along the road which goes down from Jerusalem to Gaza.' This is desert. So he arose and went. And behold, a man of Ethiopia, a eunuch of great authority under Candace the queen of the Ethiopians, who had charge of all her treasury, and had come to Jerusalem to worship, was returning. And sitting in his chariot was reading Isaiah the prophet. Then the Spirit said to Philip, 'Go near and overtake this chariot.'

"So Philip ran to him and heard him reading the prophet Isaiah, and said, 'Do you understand what you are reading?'

"And he said, 'How can I, unless someone guides me?' And he asked Philip to come up and sit with him. The place in the Scripture that he read was this:

*'He was led as a sheep to the slaughter;*
*And like a lamb silent before its shearer,*
*So He opened not His mouth.*
*In His humiliation His justice was taken away.*

*And who will declare His generation?*
*For His life is taken from the earth.'*

"So the eunuch answered Philip and said, 'I ask you, of whom does the prophet say this, of himself or of some other man?' Then Philip opened his mouth, and beginning at this Scripture, preached Jesus to him. Now as they went down the road, they came to some water. And the eunuch said, 'See, here is water. What hinders me from being baptized?'

"Then Philip said, 'If you believe with all your heart, you may.'

"And he answered and said, 'I believe that Jesus Christ is the Son of God.'

"So he commanded the chariot to stand still. And both Philip and the eunuch went down into the water, and he baptized him. Now when they came up out of the water, the Spirit of the Lord caught Philip away, so that the eunuch saw him no more; and he went on his way rejoicing. But Philip was found at Azotus. And passing through, he preached in all the cities till he came to Caesarea" (Acts 8:26-40, NKJV).

If we pray and ask to be instrumental in the salvation of souls, God and His angels will at the right time lead us to receptive people. This is part of His great cosmic plan, described in Ezekiel in the first and tenth chapters. There we find a vision of angels moving in perfect harmony with God's will as events press toward the day when our world will be fully lighted with the glory of His gospel (see Habakkuk 2:14; Revelation 18:1). Under the full blaze of this gospel light, all are free to choose their own destiny, by welcoming the truth as it is in Jesus, or rejecting it. Thus, none that truly desire salvation from God on His terms will miss that eternal blessing. Through the power of the Holy Spirit, God skillfully surmounts all the obstacles that the traditions of men and the doctrines of demons have erected as barricades against the truth (see John 14:6).

Jesus is not just one of many pathways to redemption. He is the Way, the Truth, and the Life. Thus we are ultimately either for Christ or against Him; we cannot be indulgently neutral or philosophically tolerant of the gospel. For there is no name under heaven whereby we can be saved except the name of Jesus; all other would-be redeemers are impostors (see John 10:1; Acts 4:12). And we all need redemption.

❧ ❧ ❧ ❧

Philip Follett[4] was a literature evangelist in his small California hometown. He rode through the whole town on his bicycle and over a period of several months visited every home to display his Christian books for sale. One day Philip was having unusually poor results. Somewhat discouraged, he came to a house and knocked on the door. All was quiet inside, but for some inexplicable reason Philip felt impressed to continue knocking persistently. It was as though a voice instructed him, "Do not cease knocking until someone opens this door."

Finally, after several minutes, a woman came to the door and with a puzzled and expectant expression, invited Philip, a gangly, nervous lad, to step inside. He showed his books, and she signed up to buy a substantial order.

Philip did not think much more about this visit until several years later, when a woman colporteur visited the same town and met the woman who had bought books from Philip. This same customer told the colporteur that one morning when she was about to turn on her kitchen gas stove to commit suicide she heard someone knocking at her door. She waited for the unexpected visitor to go away, but then could see that the knocking would continue until she answered the door.

When Philip introduced himself as a Christian book salesman, hope flickered in her heart that he was perhaps an unwitting messenger from God to encourage her not to give up. That is why she bought his books. Through their influence she accepted Christ and emerged victorious from the personal crisis that had nearly driven her to end her life.

Hearing this story several years later, Philip felt sure it was an angel who helped him override his usual shyness and insecurity by prompting him to knock with such tireless persistence.

"The canvasser will handle those books that bring light and strength to the soul. He will drink in the spirit of those books and will put his whole soul into the work of presenting them to the people. His strength, his courage, his success, will depend on how fully the truth presented in the books is woven into his own experience and developed in his character. When his own life is thus molded, he can go forward, representing to others the sacred truth he is handling. Imbued with the Spirit of God he will gain a deep, rich experience, and *heavenly angels will give him success in the work.*"[5]

❧ ❧ ❧

John Yuants, a young man of Papua New Guinea, had an unusually deep hunger for Bible truth. From his childhood he had learned the gospel from Protestant missionaries and had received a Bible at a Sunday School held in the jungle. John received Christ, and as he read the Bible he discovered in it many plain truths that the missionaries had not taught or did not recognize. He prayed for opportunities to bring some of these truths before his Kamblika tribes-people, but the way seemed closed up through the indifference of his people to learn more than the rudiments of the Bible at best. The impression was strong upon him, "You must tell your people the new truths that you have learned." But John did not know how to break through the barriers of their indifference. He prayed for an opening.

Tribal war drove John away for about four years, but when hostilities subsided he returned, and continued praying fervently for his people and that he might have the privilege of teaching them the rich Bible truths he was discovering. As he prayed the conviction came upon him very strongly that he must build a church. His father, a tribal chief, gave John a choice piece of land, just across the road from another church.

As John gathered materials for his building project, his father warned him that the whole village would turn against him for building another house of worship and promulgating unpopular truth from it. "You will have to worship all alone in your church," his father warned, "because none of our people will join you." As he proceeded alone with his project John received more and more abuse from the village leader and his own kinsmen.

One day he was alone in the jungle, cutting trees for the rafters of the church. He grew faint from the heavy work and was discouraged. On his way back to the village for a short rest, he met a woman who told him that two strangers in a white minibus parked under the big tree by the market wanted to talk with him.

John found the strangers, and one of them said to him: "We know about the opposition you have been facing in building this church for the truth of God. We have come to encourage you. This is a very important work that you are doing. God wants His truth to be carried to all of your people."

John wept. He couldn't help it. These were the first words of encouragement he had heard. "Work for the young people of this village. They will accept God's message," the visitor added. Then, pointing to a group of boys who were gambling under a big tree, the speaker added, "Make friends with these boys. Help them when they need food. When you are friends with them, tell them about God's truth, and they will be your first converts."

One of the men took a book out of a plastic bag. "This book, *The Desire of Ages,* is not the Bible. It was written by Ellen G. White, God's messenger to the last church. You will see how Satan opposed Jesus' work. When you are discouraged and tempted to give up, read this book. Do not put this book away. Keep it with you. Read this book with your Bible. If you do that, you will bear fruit for the Lord."

After a few more words of encouragement the stranger invited John to bow his head for prayer. Placing his hands on John's head, he offered a prayer that John testified was the most beautiful he had ever heard. Then the two men in the white bus drove away. John watched as it disappeared down the road. He was puzzled when it did not reappear beyond the bend. Hastening to the bend, he looked down the road but no vehicle was in sight. John knew that the two strangers were angels sent by God to encourage him.

John went to work with fresh courage. He read his new book with his Bible and began making friends with the gamblers to whom the angel had pointed. Soon they were helping John complete his building project. John's preaching was blessed and attracted many of the young people of the village. Since the late 1980s he has helped to prepare hundreds of people for baptism into God's full message movement, and has raised up at least five churches.[6]

"We are to be laborers together with the heavenly angels in presenting Jesus to the world. With almost impatient eagerness the angels wait for our cooperation; for man must be the channel to communicate with man. And when we give ourselves to Christ in wholehearted devotion, the angels rejoice that they may speak through our voices to reveal God's love" (*The Desire of Ages*, p. 297).

---

1. From Russell C. Thomas, *Adventure Unlimited* (Pacific Press, 1988), pp. 22-24.

2. Adapted from adult Sabbath School lesson quarterly (Pacific Press, 1996), first quarter 1997.

3. From Arthur S. Maxwell, *Bedtime Stories* (Pacific Press, 1976), vol. 4, pp. 157-160.

4. At the time of this writing, Philip Follett is a vice-president of the General Conference of Seventh-day Adventists in Silver Spring, Maryland.

5. Ellen G. White, *Colporteur Ministry* (Pacific Press, 1990), p. 112, emphasis supplied.

6. Adapted from LaVerne Tucker, *Miracles of the Message* (The Quiet Hour, 1997), pp. 93-96.

# CHAPTER FIVE

# *Healing Angels*

Wherever Jesus walked, throngs of suffering people came to Him for deliverance from their infirmities of mind and body. Jesus delighted in placing His healing touch on them. He went "about in all Galilee, teaching in their synagogues, and proclaiming the gospel of the kingdom, and healing every kind of disease and every kind of sickness among the people. And the news about Him went out into all Syria; and they brought to Him all that were ill, taken with various diseases and pains, demoniacs, epileptics, paralytics; and He healed them" (Matthew 4:23, 24, NASB).

Angels serve as living extensions of God's will. Their hands and faculties are at His command. It is no wonder then that we should find them frequently acting as agents to heal and restore those who reach out to God and for whom special prayer is offered.

Cyril Miller[1] writes:

"Traveling late one night on a narrow rural highway, I met with a near-fatal accident. A semi truck swung

69

into my lane with blinding lights and then swerved sharply to the left to make a quick turn into a driveway, thus leaving the trailer squarely in my lane.

"Automatically applying the brakes, I jerked my car to the right toward the ditch, but it was too late. Crashing headlong into the trailer, I found myself pinned by the motor, which had been thrust into the front seat.

"I awakened to hear the excitement of people trying to free me from the wreckage. One man was shouting, 'We will have to cut off his foot to get him out.' I pleaded, 'Please do not cut off my foot,' and prayed, 'Dear Lord, don't let them cut off my foot.'

"The motor was jacked up, thereby freeing me, and the top of my automobile was torn away with a 'jaws of life' rescue machine. Then I was removed, placed inside a helicopter, and flown to a major hospital in the city nearby.

"Still conscious upon arrival, I asked the attending nurse for pen and paper. I gave her a message for the doctor, which simply said, 'Please do not amputate my foot.' Immediately I went unconscious and stayed that way for nearly a month. While in a coma, it seemed as if I was in a dark cave. I could hear people talking but could see nothing. I even heard the doctors and nurses say, 'He isn't going to make it.'

"In addition to a crushed right foot and lower leg, I had multiple fractures in my arm, which was never set; crushed ribs; flayed lungs; and other injuries. Additional complications resulted when I developed bacterial pneumonia and a staphylococcic infection in my wounds during the time I was unconscious.

"Four weeks later I awakened to discover that God had miraculously spared my life as an answer to many prayers by friends everywhere. One night, when it appeared that I might not live through the night, three ministers came and anointed me as the Bible instructs in James 5:14.

"From then on I made steady progress, except that I still had many life support tubes all over my body. Tubes were in my arms for medication, my stomach for nourishment, my bladder for voiding, my lungs for draining, and my throat for breathing.

"Actually, I was on respirator support during the four weeks of unconsciousness and the fifth week after awakening. One evening the pulmonary specialist came by and said, 'Your lungs may not come back.'

"I asked, 'What does that mean?'

"He replied, 'You will be short of breath the rest of your life.'

"Though unable at this time to breathe without the respirator, I didn't recognize how bad the prognosis was. Engulfed in deep depression, I thought, *I'll never be the same again, not being able to preach or even talk without difficulty.*

"A few evenings later, a young man whom I had never seen before, came to my room. In a very assuring, authoritative voice, he said, 'I have special ears; I can hear things that no one else can hear.'

"As he began to place the stethoscope on my chest, I asked, 'What do you hear?'

"He answered, 'I hear a free flow of air through every lobe of your lungs.'

"I looked out in the hall and saw Joyce, who is now my wife, waiting and motioned for her to come into the room. After introducing her to the young man, I told her what he had just told me by saying, 'He has special ears and can hear things that no one else can hear.' He repeated the same words again: 'I hear a free flow of air through every lobe of his lungs,' and then he left quickly.

"Later, my sister, her pastor husband, and my daughter came to visit me. I told them about the young man and what he had said. Since they had stayed very close—almost day and night during those critical weeks—and knew virtually everyone who came in and out of the room, they asked, 'Who was he? What did he look like?'

"I replied, 'He has never been here before. I can't describe him—except that he was a nice looking young man.'

"My daughter answered, 'Dad, those are the very words Ellen

White used to describe her guardian angel—a nice looking young man.' I thought that my daughter was just trying to encourage me, so I smiled and acknowledged her answer.

"However, about a week later, I was reading in the book of Mark about the women who went to Jesus' tomb on the Resurrection morning and found it empty. It says that they looked inside the tomb and there sat a young man.

"I said, 'Wait a minute, what translation is this? I thought the Bible said it was an angel.' Quickly turning to the front, I discovered it was the *King James Version*. So I turned to the other Gospels, where I discovered that the person in the tomb is called an angel.

"I began to reflect upon all of this. Health professionals simply do not talk like the young man who said, 'I have special ears, and I can hear things that no one else can hear.' Also, my pulmonary specialist visited me about a week later and said, 'Well, it looks as though your lungs are going to be OK,' and I thought, *I already know that.*

"Then I reasoned: If angels appeared as young men in Bible times, and if Ellen White described her guardian angel as a 'nice-looking young man,' then I may have seen my guardian angel. I had never seen this young man before, and I have never seen him since this unusual experience.

"I was telling a friend of mine about my remarkable encounter and the conviction that it must have been an angel, and he replied, 'Well, Cyril, you may have seen your guardian angel. If he doesn't send you a bill, it probably was.'

"One of my attending physicians, an infection specialist, the one who had said, 'He isn't going to make it,' later acknowledged that I was healed by 'divine intervention.'

"I thank God for saving my life and restoring my health. I also thank Him for dispatching one of His 'ministering spirits' to assure me and give me peace of mind that I would be all right, at a time when I most needed support.

"It has been about four years since my accident, and I am able to routinely perform my administrative and ministerial work, which I greatly enjoy—especially preaching God's Word on Sabbaths and in evangelistic meetings."

❦ ❦ ❦ ❦

Before we share more stories of divinely granted healing, a few words of caution. As children of God, we must learn not to be simplistic. Not in every case of sickness and injury does God heal, even if we exercise the strongest faith and send to Him the most earnest petitions. Sometimes the summit of faith requires that we accept life-long affliction.

Why? For one thing, it places us on solid ground to comfort any who must bear debilitating infirmities. For another, affliction can serve to keep us humbly dependent on God.

That's the effect that affliction had on the apostle Paul. This great servant of God was instrumental in bringing healing to many (see Acts 19:11, 12). On the island of Malta where Paul was shipwrecked, a viper that darted out of some firewood he had gathered bit him. The islanders and passengers from the wrecked vessel were sure that this viper-bite was a judgment from the "gods." They said, " 'No doubt this man is a murderer, whom, though he has escaped the sea, yet justice does not allow to live.' But he shook off the creature into the fire and suffered no harm" (Acts 28:4, 5).

This very circumstance led the superstitious islanders to believe that Paul was a god, thus opening the way for him to be used by God to heal the father of Publius, one of the island's leading citizens. That, in turn, quickly inspired the confidence of the people, who brought their sick in droves to Paul, through whom God sent healing in abundance. We may be certain that, as a result, many turned from pagan superstition to Christ.

But then what about Paul's own health? In 2 Corinthians we learn that he had a thorn in the flesh that caused him physical suffering and debility. Did this great healer not have influence with God to obtain the restoration he so longed for? "And lest I should be exalted above measure by the abundance of the revelations, a thorn in the flesh was given to me, a messenger of Satan to buffet me, lest I be exalted above measure" (2 Corinthians 12:7).

Paul did not just blithely accept his "thorn in the flesh." It was a great trial to him, and it imposed seemingly severe limitations on him that he feared would hinder his work for God.

"Concerning this thing I pleaded with the Lord three times that it might depart from me, and He said to me, 'My grace is sufficient for you, for My strength is made perfect in weakness.' Therefore most gladly I will rather boast in my infirmities, that the power of Christ may rest upon me. Therefore I take pleasure in infirmities, in reproaches, in needs, in persecutions, in distresses, for Christ's sake. For when I am weak, then I am strong" (2 Corinthians 12:8-10).

Paul's experience helps us to see that Christian faith is not a magic wand that brings immediate fulfillment of our every wish. " 'We must through many tribulations enter the kingdom of God' " (Acts 14:22). Matthew Henry, the great Bible commentator, stated it thus: "Extraordinary afflictions are not always the punishment of extraordinary sins, but sometimes the trial of extraordinary graces. Sanctified afflictions are spiritual promotions."

❦ ❦ ❦ ❦

My own life [writes Brian Jones] was vitally affected by the witness of a godly woman who suffered one of the most dreaded of physical handicaps—blindness. Grace Jajeh, a Lebanese-American Christian, had been blind from early childhood. Converted to Christ in her early teens, she was spellbound by the accounts of His healing activity recorded in the Gospels. Grace often thought, *How wonderful it would be if only Jesus would give me back my eyesight.*

She often prayed for this blessing. Though her sight did not return, Grace still maintained a cheerful faith. Yet at times she would be overwhelmed with sorrow over her unchanged condition. Grace was tempted to think that God was not hearing her prayers. She wondered, too, whether she was doing something to displease Him, thus hindering His power to heal. She drew some consolation from the verse, "For we walk by faith, and not by sight" (2 Corinthians 5:7).

Grace's cheerful disposition and sincere praise for Christ, made her a channel of blessing to many. Yet the undercurrent of sadness in her heart continued. One Monday morning Grace came to the adult school for the blind. An unusual joy beamed from her face as she launched irrepressibly into her story.

"Last night I had a dream," she announced. "An angel came to me in my dream—a bright angel, glorious with heaven's light. He asked me, 'Grace, if you can have one of two blessings, either to have your eyesight back in this life, or to win a soul for Jesus, which would you choose?' I woke up," Grace said, "shouting, 'A soul for Jesus, Lord, a soul for Jesus!' "

I have no doubt that her vibrant faith added many souls to God's kingdom. I know that Grace's testimony that Monday morning turned the tide in my life toward the Savior, whose claims on my heart I had been rather ambivalent about.

Many people who loved the Lord during their earthly lives will see and hear and walk for the first time in heaven, when Jesus comes. "Then the eyes of the blind shall be opened, and the ears of the deaf shall be unstopped . . . and the ransomed of the Lord shall return, and come to Zion with singing, with everlasting joy on their heads. They shall obtain joy and gladness, and sorrow and sighing shall flee away" (Isaiah 35:5, 10).

❧ ❧ ❧ ❧

The body is the temple of the Holy Spirit. We are not our own because we are bought with a price. We must glorify God in our bodies (see Philippians 1:20; 1 Corinthians 3:16; 6:19, 20). The beauty and far-reaching significance of this truth are fascinatingly illustrated in the experience of the Barbosas. Youthful, attractive, and energetic, Pastor Alfredo Barbosa and his wife, Aurea, were among the most productive soul-winners in Brazil. Through their dedication to God the churches prospered wherever they served. Besides being a good pastor, Alfredo was an excellent evangelist, and Aurea complemented his work exceptionally well.

Responding to an invitation to move to Corumba near the Bolivian border, the Barbosas looked forward to their new assignment. On their way to Corumba, Aurea and her husband bought some salve at a pharmacy to treat a slight skin irritation that had developed on Aurea's arm. For a while the salve helped, as did some calcium injections from a local doctor. But then Aurea's skin problem reappeared, only this time more severely. After several months of various treatments that seemed to work for a while, Aurea had fresh and increasingly extensive outbreaks of the rash. So the Barbosas determined to get a definitive diagnosis and effective treatment. But the best place to find that help was in Sao Paulo, 1,200 miles away.

Pastors' salaries were small and health care benefits were limited. So the Barbosas decided to stop first at a hot spring, Aguas Caliente, whose waters were famous for their healing properties, especially for skin diseases. This hot spring was in a dense, humid jungle, with nothing but the most primitive facilities available. Pastor Barbosa and his wife camped by the spring in the sultry weather. The treatments were extremely uncomfortable for Aurea, but she suffered through them as best she could. To compound her misery she contracted malaria in the jungle, and had to deal with alternating fever and chills along with her itchy, burning rash.

The Barbosas feared that Aurea's disease was the dreaded *fogo selvagem,* savage fire, which eventually covers the whole body with a sheath of fiery, oozing blisters. At that time no cure was known for this disease, and most of its victims died after months or years of horrifying misery.

Eventually, the Barbosas' worst fears were confirmed. Aurea was indeed suffering from savage fire. And she was dying from it. Rather than try to press on to Sao Paulo, Pastor Barbosa called for the elders at the Corumba church to provide help in getting Aurea back home. Two women from the church came by train to assist. Trains passed through the area of Aguas Caliente only once a day. So the Barbosas and their two friends from Corumba spent a night in the jungle, planning to leave the next day.

In the morning Aurea awoke to express more hope than she had felt for months. She said to her husband and friends, "I've never been one to believe in dreams, but I want to believe in last night's dream with every fiber of my being. In my dream I heard a voice say, 'Aurea, you are going to get well. Aurea, you're going to get well!' This voice kept repeating these words in the most reassuring manner. Afterward I saw both of you dear sisters coming to help me. I even saw the dresses you were wearing— exactly the same dresses you have on now. I want to believe an angel was sent to comfort me, and your presence here is a sign that I shall recover."

The four prayed together, led by Pastor Barbosa. Then came the painful work of transporting Aurea back home. Covered with painful sores and unable to straighten out her legs lest it tear her flesh, she found every movement excruciatingly painful. It would take a book to narrate all the additional trials that the Barbosas faced in their search for a cure, including medicine that had no effect, doctors who were powerless to offer relief, and hot water treatments that did not work. When and how would it all end?

The Barbosas suffered growing ostracism as Aurea's dreaded disease progressed. Her whole body turned into a mass of flaming, scaly sores that made her look like the victim of third degree burns. A hospital in Sao Paulo for *fogo selvagem* patients resigned itself to the probability that Aurea's case was fatal, as no successful treatment had been discovered. Moreover, they would not accept her as a patient except in the short term, since she was not from the state of Sao Paulo. Because of Aurea's condition, Pastor Barbosa could not find anyone willing to rent an apartment or garage for their lodging.

Finally they were able to find some good friends in the area of Sao Paulo who provided them with lodging and care. Then Pastor Barbosa was invited to carry on his ministerial work in Sao Paulo, making it possible for the family to be together again, as well as have access to medical facilities. For many months, friends in Corumba looked after the Barbosas' children.

Before returning to Corumba to pick up his children and move their household belongings to Sao Paulo, Pastor Barbosa went to the town of Campo Grande to visit Aurea's parents and sell her cattle to help pay their medical debts. While in Campo Grande, Pastor Barbosa looked up the street one day and saw a tall black woman getting into the passenger seat of a car. How he discerned this, Barbosa could not say, but to him her blackness did not appear to be the natural pigmentation of her race, but the result of some special condition. On an inexplicable impulse he ran up the street to the car and breathlessly asked the driver, "Why is the woman next to you so black?" He shocked himself by this question. Barbosa was not a racist or a bigot, nor was he an idly inquisitive man. Normally he was quite reserved, and it certainly was not polite or reasonable to make such a query, but he felt irresistibly compelled to do it.

Fortunately, the man behind the wheel was friendly. He replied, "Oh, she had *fogo selvagem,* savage fire, but is completely cured now. Her present color is a temporary effect of the remedy."

"Cured? But how? I've never heard of anyone being cured of *fogo selvagem.* My wife has it, and I need this remedy for her," Barbosa blurted out, frantic and excited. For the first time in months, hope sprang up in his heart. *Could my wife's dream be true? Will she really be cured?* he wondered. *Did an angel guide me up this street at this time and prompt me to rush up to this car with my brash question?*

"My wife was paralyzed in bed with *fogo selvagem,* ready to die," explained the stranger. "The man who provided the remedy lives about fifty miles from here."

Pastor Barbosa made an appointment with his newfound friend, to learn more about how his wife was healed. As he heard more of the story that evening in the man's home, Barbosa marveled. The most advanced medical experts in Rio de Janeiro and Sao Paulo could do nothing for savage fire, but now he was learning that Isidoro Jamar, an alcoholic pharmacist in a small jungle village on the Paraguayan border, had developed a cure that he alone knew.

Getting accurate directions, Barbosa and a fellow pastor went out to the village and found a semi-stupefied Dr. Jamar willing to sell them a batch of medicine, which he had to concoct as they waited. Dr. Jamar closely guarded his formula and would not let anyone watch him select and combine the ingredients. He would sell the formula to no one, believing that if he did so, some huge pharmaceutical firm would patent it and make it available only to the wealthy who could afford the medicine. His reasoning might have been faulty, but he refused to divulge the chemical formula for his nearly absolute cure. A large amount of pitch in the formula turned those who used it the color of ebony, which remained until new skin replaced the diseased, sloughed-off tissue.

True to Aurea's dream, and the promised effect of the medicine, she was cured in several weeks. Soon Aurea was again able to help her husband in his soul-winning endeavors and care for her children.

Using the medicine left over from the stock they had purchased from Dr. Jamar, they applied it to sufferers of savage fire who came to them for aid. From time to time Pastor Barbosa would renew his supply by going out to see Dr. Jamar, because more and more savage fire patients were coming to the Barbosas for treatment. Unable to turn anyone away, they built a small clinic for these patients. Soon it grew so crowded that they had to seek funding for a larger clinic. The Barbosas made no profits for their service, but did much of the work at their own expense, many of their patients being utterly destitute and some outcast like lepers. Caring church members and others, recognizing the altruistic motives of the Barbosas, helped build a well-equipped hospital in Campo Grande, Brazil. It was called Hospital Matogrossense do Penfigo, which began as a 25-bed facility, and was shortly afterwards expanded to a 150-bed capacity. There, hundreds of savage fire sufferers received loving care and healing from their once untreatable disease.

Two weeks before his death from tuberculosis, Dr. Jamar gave the formula for his medicine to Pastor Barbosa. He saw that the pastor and his wife were using the medicine as benefactors to humanity and not for personal profit or aggrandizement. Soon the medicine began to be manufactured under safe laboratory conditions and distributed widely through private and government agencies for sufferers of this formerly incurable disease. Pharmaceutical researchers in Brazil retained the key elements of Dr. Jamar's formula, improving it in several ways, including the removal of its cancer-causing pitch. In honor of its inventor they named the medicine *Jamarsan.*

Often Alfredo and Aurea Barbosa thought afterwards that, had she not been afflicted with this terrible disease which almost took her life, they would never have become aware of the cure and would not have been led to develop a medical ministry for its many sufferers. How overjoyed they would have been if one anointing service had healed Aurea in the early days of her affliction. But how much more grateful they were in the end to have been instrumental in helping save the lives of thousands of victims of savage fire through the mysterious chain of providences that led to their finding the remedy. The secret would have died with its inventor if the Barbosas had not been people of such broad and unselfish vision.

King David wrote in a psalm, "It is good for me that I have been afflicted, that I may learn Your statutes" (Psalm 119:71). And the apostle Paul wrote, "Blessed be the God and Father of our Lord Jesus Christ, the Father of mercies and the God of all comfort, who comforts us in all our tribulation, that we may be able to comfort those who are in any trouble, with the comfort which we ourselves are comforted by God. . . . We had the sentence of death in ourselves, that we should not trust in ourselves but in God who raises the dead, who delivered us from so great a death, and does deliver us; in whom we trust that He will still deliver us" (2 Corinthians 1:3, 4, 9, 10).

❦ ❦ ❦ ❦

We close this chapter with another story showing an angel's part in healing a man who used his restored health to become a partner with angels in leading others to the Great Physician, Jesus, for the healing of the soul from its ultimate affliction—sin.

Vasele Lupu looked up from his hospital bed into the eyes of his son, Benone. "It's not good news," he said quietly. "The doctor says the cancer might have spread. But I have placed my life in God's hands. I am ready to live or die as He wills."

The two men prayed together in the hospital room in Bucharest, Romania. Then Benone left. Two days later when he returned to visit his father, he found him preparing to go home.

"What happened?" the younger man asked. "You were so ill!"

"I may have been dreaming," the elder man told his son. "But after you left I saw an intense light at the foot of my bed. A man standing in the light told me that God had a work for me to do. Later I asked my roommate if he had seen a bright light or heard a voice during the night, but he had seen and heard nothing. Surely I have been visited by an angel!"

Lupu, now healed and full of vitality, asked God to show him the ministry God had for him. He began visiting the prison in Bucharest, where he had spent several years as a prisoner for his faith during Communist times. He recognized many of the guards, and he remembered the insults that he had endured from guards and prisoners alike because of his faith. One guard recognized him and hurled new insults at him.

Lupu began sharing with the prisoners the message of hope in Christ. The guard who had insulted him listened to Lupu's testimony. His heart was touched, and he accepted Christ as his Savior.

But the guard's wife was angry about his decision. "How can an intelligent person believe there is a God?" she demanded. Then she challenged her husband. "Do you see this plant? It has never blossomed. If your God can make this plant bloom, then I will believe!"

Later that day the woman walked into the room where the barren plant sat. She stared at it amazed, for the plant was blooming! Faith blossomed in her heart, and she joined her husband to worship God and later followed him in baptism.

Lupu thanks God for giving him a special work to do.[2]

Whether, you are sick or well, healed or bearing the cross of an infirmity, remember that angels wish to join you as partners in making known the Savior. Through His gospel all disease will ultimately be banished, and He will take His redeemed to a kingdom where the inhabitants will never say, "I am sick," but will revel in the abundance of health that pervades their bodies and souls. In the meantime, Christ will bear your infirmities, either by removing them, or as is sometimes more precious, by giving you grace to endure them, so that whether by life or by death, His love may be magnified in you.

---

1. At the time of this writing, Cyril Miller serves as vice-president for evangelism and global mission at the North American Division of the Seventh-day Adventist Church in Silver Spring, Maryland. He is also chair of the Voice of Prophecy board of directors.
2. From J. H. Zachary, international evangelism coordinator for The Quiet Hour radio broadcast.

# CHAPTER SIX

# Angel Teachers

We have seen that angels are versatile and have multiple tasks to perform, which they carry out with speed, accuracy, and skill that baffles our understanding. But angels perform no greater or more vital work than that of teaching. Their chief aim is to guide us into knowledge of Christ (see Zechariah 1:9-15). Consider their active role in Revelation as communicators of divine truth, sent from the courts of heaven to instruct human hearts (see Revelation 1:1; 8:13; 11:15).

The following stories illustrate this teaching role in amazing ways. Missionary Betty Cott, who, with her husband, Alfred, took the gospel to inland Guyana, tells her own story:

"It was with a feeling of awe that we approached Owkwa's village. Would our findings substantiate what we had heard? After the usual Indian greetings of handshakes, hugs, and friendly blowing in our ears, the villagers asked, 'May we see your Bibles?' We were astonished at this question. This was the first time any

Indians, upon greeting us, had manifested an interest in the Book that means so much to us.

"When we showed them the three Bibles we had brought, their eyes sparkled with delight. 'You our missionaries,' they affirmed.

" 'How do you know we are missionaries?' Alfred asked.

" 'Owkwa say you have black book from country called England, so we know when right people come.'

"We opened our Bibles, and sure enough, all three had been printed in England. Could it be that the Lord had been preparing these people for our arrival while we were yet children? It had been years since Owkwa had had his dreams. We figured it must have been 1902.

"Chief Promi, the son of Owkwa, had taught the people well. This was the cleanest village we had ever entered. The people were clothed more fully than any other Indians we had encountered, and their customs were more sanitary than those of other nations we had known.

"One thing that greatly astonished us was their knowledge of the English language. When we questioned them as to where they had obtained this knowledge, they replied, 'Owkwa teach us. Angel teach Owkwa.' They were quite familiar with such English Bible terms as Holy Bible, hallelujah, New Jerusalem, Holy Spirit, 'body is the temple,' Jesus, heavenly Father, great light, Satan, sorrow, trial. We had a common ground of communication as far as Bible knowledge was concerned.

"Chief Promi, with the rest of the village trailing along behind, escorted us to a clean, whitewashed hut. 'We build for you,' he proudly told us. 'Take us many moons.' "

Deeply grateful for this provision, the Cotts settled in without delay. Soon they had a visit from several village girls, who clapped their hands outside the hut, the customary way of "knocking." "Sister, brother," they called.

They graciously presented to the Cotts some bananas, sweet potatoes, and cassava. The missionaries were astonished to see that the roots had been scrubbed clean—something the other

Indians never did because of their superstitious fear of water.

Mrs. Cott writes:

" 'Why did you clean the vegetables?' I asked the girls.

"Madeline, Chief Promi's niece, flashed me a bright smile, 'Angel told Owkwa, we wash food. Clean, clean.'

"We had just finished eating when Chief Promi came to the door to inform us that the Indians were gathering for a meeting. Hastily we gathered up the projector, the sheet for a screen, trumpet, and saxophone, and made our way to the whitewashed church. As we entered, I was astonished to see that everything was so clean and noted that there was a lovely bouquet of orchids on the rostrum. This was the first time I had seen flowers in a jungle church. Wildflowers are so common there that the Indians don't bother to make bouquets of them.

"We draped our large projection sheet across a rope provided for that purpose. To begin the meeting the Indians sang a song in English that I had never heard before. It sounded like heavenly music to us. The words, sung with much feeling, went something like this: 'Holy, holy, God almighty; we love dear Jesus. We long to hear the angels sing someday in New Jerusalem.'

"Alfred asked Promi to offer the prayer.

"As the people knelt, I couldn't help noticing the children. With the older ones they bowed with much reverence, their hands tightly covering their eyes. All during the prayer I didn't hear a movement. After Promi started to pray, the congregation joined in, repeating his words of praise and petition. The reverent manner of these worshipers stirred us to the very depths.

"Following this prayer Alfred made some introductory remarks, and I flashed the first picture on the screen. Immediately Madeline jumped up, face flushed and eyes aglow, exclaiming with elation, 'That's what my grandfather said the missionaries would show us.' The picture was one of Jesus and the angels.

"The next picture was of the table set before the saints in New Jerusalem.

" 'Ah, ah!' Promi exclaimed. 'That table Owkwa saw—plenty, plenty long.'

"Later on in the evening we showed a picture of the creation of the animals. Madeline's young husband, a great hunter, remarked, 'Grandfather told us that when we go to heaven, we see tiger and lamb sleeping together. That's what I want to see.'

"The last slide of the evening was of Christ coming in the clouds of glory. When the people saw this, they all cried out excitedly, 'Owkwa tell us this! Angel tell Owkwa.' In order to get the story straight before showing any more slides, Alfred sought out Promi the next morning, notebook in hand. 'Please tell me as nearly as you can what it was your father saw.'

"Promi began, 'One day my father having a meeting; he suddenly no talk more. His eyes like glass. He look to heaven, but no breathe, though standing upright. I think he dead.'

" 'How long did he stand this way?' Alfred asked.

" 'Until sun high overhead. Everybody afraid. No one see this before. Some people cry. Some try put him down on floor. No could move him. He stay just like rock.' Promi talked in subdued tones as he described this scene. He continued, 'Finally, he take deep breath and blink his eyes. I ask him, 'Papa, you sick?' He tell me and all the people that he no sick; but he see some wonderful things. Then he describe heaven to us as we saw in pictures last night. He tell about beautiful place—long table and all. Papa say heaven bright place. He wish not to come back to earth. This earth bad place. He want to stay in heaven. Here we work with knives and cutlasses to live, but not in heaven.'

" 'That's amazing,' Alfred said. 'Did the angel come more than once?'

" 'Angel come plenty, plenty times.'

" 'When did the angel first come?'

" 'Plenty, plenty moons ago. Me little boy. But me remember. Papa when he become chief, he pray and talk to Great Spirit. Many, many days and nights he pray. He tell Great Spirit, he like to make his people good. Then angel come and talk to him.'

" 'What did the angel tell him first?'

" 'Papa had three wives; angel tell him he must have only one. Owkwa tell two wives to go. Wives mad; try to poison Owkwa. He tell all his people must be clean, have only one wife. Angel tell Papa one night that we must keep seventh day holy. Angel say Sabbath begin sundown Friday. Time holy until sun go down again. No work then. Eat little food on Sabbath. Much food make one too sleepy.'

" 'How did you know which day was Sabbath?'

" 'Angel say to Papa which day.'

" 'How did you keep track of the days of the week from then on?'

"Promi flashed a bright smile. 'We make string from cotton Mamma grew. We tie knots. Big one for Sabbath. Easy.'

" 'Where did you worship before you built the church?'

" 'Papa's hut. He make all clean and nice. Papa tell buckman what angel say to him. Buckman good and kind, like Owkwa. They work together to build church. Me help too. When church finish, Owkwa say need somebody to help keep church clean. Must put pretty flowers in church.' "

Next, Mrs. Cott asked the women of the village to assemble for some instruction in healthful living. She wrote:

"I showed them some posters about clean and unclean meats, especially emphasizing that blood should not be an article of food. I had seen many Indians on the trail kill an animal and then drain the blood to drink it.

"Noticing grins spread over the faces of all the women, I wondered what I had said wrong. But at this juncture Madeline could contain herself no longer. She jumped to her feet, a broad smile on her face. 'But, sister, we don't eat blood,' she said excitedly. 'No unclean meats. No pig, no rabbit, no rats, no fish without scales.' She sat down breathless.

"I must have looked my astonishment, for she added, 'Owkwa tell us No. Angel tell Owkwa.'

"Then I tried a different approach. I told them they shouldn't make *cassere.* Again, grins spread over their faces.

"'All right,' I said, laughing. 'You don't make *cassere* [native beer].'

"'Owkwa say, make drunk. Dirty. People no use,' several responded.

"When I demonstrated to them how to give water treatments, Margy, Promi's wife, informed me that they had treated their sick like that for many, many moons.

"When I went back to our cottage I said to Alfred, 'What can I teach these people? Everything I've tried to tell them, they are already doing.'

"'I have had much the same experience,' Alfred said. 'Instead of us teaching them, they are teaching us. Their reverence and sincerity certainly surpass anything we have seen back home.'

"'Yes, I hear them praying and singing at four o'clock in the morning. Promi told me today the details about the judgment and the seven last plagues, just as we believe them. He said the earth would be destroyed by fire and hail—he called it *piroto,* which means "shot." This, he said, would be thrown down from heaven on the wicked.'

"One day Madeline told us that Owkwa informed them that he would die. The angel had instructed him that he would not live to see the missionaries. He admonished them to be faithful; but also said that some would backslide. We found this to be true. Some had not remained faithful. It was clear that Owkwa did not flatter his people, but patiently exhorted and warned them. "On discovering that the word *Owkwa* meant 'great light,' Alfred asked Promi who had named his father. 'The angel tell my father,' Promi replied, 'his name be Owkwa.'

"These Indians had a song of the setting sun. They would sing it as they watched the sun go down and would think of the New Jerusalem, comparing the sorrows and trials of this dark world with the glories of that heavenly land where there is no night; and they would weep as they sang.

"And so it went all the days of our stay with these remarkable people. One truth after another they brought up that Owkwa had taught them. It was hard to tear ourselves away. We felt that we had experienced a taste of heaven. We remember the passage found in Joel 2:28: ' "And it shall come to pass afterward, that I will pour out My Spirit upon all flesh." '

"That the above prophecy is meeting a striking fulfillment today has been indelibly impressed on our minds as a result of our thrilling encounter with the Davis Indians. It must be evident to all who are marking the rapid progress of the message in these last days that God is using more than ordinary means for the promulgation of His truth."[1]

❧ ❧ ❧ ❧

Pastor Elwyn Martin, missionary to Papua New Guinea, relates this fascinating account as reported to him by a fellow missionary, Haru, a Papuan whom he trained in soul winning.

"Haru and his companions took a missionary trip by canoe down the Turama River. In each village along the way, they spent a day or so, sometimes more. One day, as they rounded a bend in the river they saw several small canoes half a mile or more ahead. Some of these canoes disappeared into the overhanging undergrowth on the riverbank. Reaching the spot, they found a small opening into another tributary called the Wamuri River. However, by the time they had found the opening the canoes were nowhere in sight.

"All except Haru were in favor of going on, for there was no village in sight. However, Haru said, 'Did not Pastor Martin tell us we were not to bypass one village? We must find where the canoe people came from.' So they traveled up the small river for several miles till at last they came to a village.

"I should explain that the Turama villages were not villages in the true sense of the word, for there was only one house, called a *dubu,* which could be one or two hundred yards in length. One I saw was almost four hundred yards long. Inside lived men and women, boys and girls, pigs and dogs, and on the sides of the dubu, about shoulder high, were racks and racks of human skulls, grim reminders of cannibalistic feasts.

"On reaching the village, Haru's band was surprised to find that it appeared deserted. Soon, however, they found that the people were inside enjoying a feast of human flesh. As soon as it could be arranged, Haru gathered the people together in a little clearing, where he produced a Picture Roll and began telling the story of the One who had changed him from a heathen to an ambassador for Jesus Christ.

"Haru said that he had been speaking only about five minutes through an interpreter, when an old man, whom he recognized immediately as a chief, came in and sat among the listeners. Almost immediately the chief jumped to his feet and said, 'Take notice of this, my people. It's true, it's true.'

"Haru continued his story only to be interrupted intermittently by the chief, saying, 'It's true, it's true. Take notice of it, my people.'

"Haru was impatient and almost exasperated because of the frequent interruptions.

"When the meeting concluded Haru walked over to the chief and said, 'Have you heard this story before?'

"The chief answered, 'No, never, but I know it's true.'

" 'Then somebody must have told you this story.'

" 'No, never.' The chief was positive, but he emphasized, 'It's true, it's true, I know it's true.'

"Almost in desperation Haru said, 'Listen, if you know it's true, then how do you know?'

" 'My name is Doni. Some weeks ago I was asleep in this big dubu and was awakened to see a man clothed in garments so bright and shining that I could not look upon them. This man said, "Doni, you are to leave your village and go back into the mountains and build yourself a house there. If you do so I will come again." '

"Doni was so impressed that early next morning he called his people together and told them what he had seen and heard. He gave orders for the people to go back into the mountains and build him a house. The villagers had never heard of anything so ridiculous and thought he must have become mentally deranged, but they dared not disobey his commands, for when a village chief speaks his people do not ask the reason why.

"A few days later, when the house was completed, Doni was ready to take his wife and three children to the mountains. They objected strongly, but they, too, eventually obeyed.

"The very first night that Doni and his family were in their new home the visitor came again, clothed in the same white, bright garments, which Doni described as 'brighter and much whiter than the noonday sun.' The visitor said, 'Doni, tomorrow you are to leave your house and return to your village. You are to destroy all your pigs and, if you do so, I will come again.'

"To carry out this command required more sacrifice and more faith because his pigs were his wealth. Men bought their wives and their land with pigs and could even settle differences with their enemies by exchanging pigs, but, as he said, 'More than anything in the world I wanted to see that visitor again.'

"Early the next morning Doni returned to his village and had all seventy of his pigs destroyed. His people, after this, thought that surely he was 'long, long' (mad). For days they feasted on swine's flesh, but Doni refused to eat or touch any of it and would not allow his wife and children to eat it.

"Back in Doni's mountain home that night the visitor came again, dressed in the same way. This time he said, 'Doni, tomorrow you are to go out to your garden and bring in sufficient food, for the next day you are not to go to your garden. You are not to go fishing or hunting in the bush, but remain in your house. If you do that, I will come again.'

"That day at home was the most wonderful day he had ever spent, because he felt that he was in the presence of the visitor, even though he could not see him during the daylight hours.

"In the darkness after that wonderful day, the visitor said, 'Doni, tomorrow you are to go out to your garden and bring in produce sufficient for several days, place it outside your door, but do not use it. If you do that, I will come again.'

"Doni said that by this time he was prepared to do anything, for more than anything in the world he wanted to see the visitor again. He could hardly wait for the next visit. Yet he wondered why he should be told to bring the garden produce and not use it, but leave it outside his door.

"That night, when the produce was outside the door in several bundles called *billums* (woven string bags), the visitor came again and said, 'Doni, tomorrow morning you are to go outside your house. There you will find a measure by which you are to measure your garden produce. If you do that, I will come again.'

"Sure enough, outside his house the next morning there was a measure, perhaps a little different from the types we are used to. It was in the form of a pole about four inches thick and about fourteen feet long. Doni began with his *kau kau* (sweet potatoes) and put the first one at the first mark. Then he noticed that there was another mark, so he put one at that, and another and another, up to five, six, seven, eight, and nine. Then another mark appeared right near the end of the pole. It was separated, quite a distance from the other nine marks. So he put a *kau kau* on that mark too, and then he began from the beginning to do the same thing again. Not only did he measure out his *kau kau* like this but also his pineapples, pawpaws, bananas, and in fact all his garden produce.

"There he left it all, not knowing the reason why.

"That night the visitor came again and said, 'Doni, the food alongside marks one, two, three, four, five, six, seven, eight, and nine is yours. Do what you like with it, but the food alongside mark ten is mine. It is to be put in a *billum,* but otherwise is not to be touched. If you do that, I will come again.'

"In the dead of night as Doni was waiting for his visitor to come, suddenly the whole area seemed to be lit up. Within moments the same bright shining visitor stood in his doorway. Doni said he always had to cover his eyes with his hands because of the dazzling brightness. This time the visitor said, 'Doni, tomorrow afternoon you and your family are to gather up all your food, and mine too, and return to your village. When you arrive, my ambassador will be there. Give him the food that is mine, and listen very carefully to every word that he says because you will know it's true, it's true.'

"It was then that Doni handed Haru the *billum* of food. Doni, in telling Haru the story, said, 'That's why I kept on telling my people, "It's true, it's true." I know it's true.' "

Recognizing the importance of this encounter with Doni's tribe, Pastor Martin set sail almost immediately for the Turama area with Haru and his wife and family. He tells the story of this experience:

"Haru wanted to return to be with 'his people.' I hadn't planned for this trip but felt that since I had heard Haru's story, it must take priority.

"We found our way up the Turama and then up the Wamuri.

"I shall never forget my first night at Doni's village. I warned Kaura, Haru's wife, and his children not to step off the boat, for after all we were among cannibals. While conducting my first meeting that night, I found it difficult to tolerate the stench of human flesh being cooked in the bamboo cooking tubes. Stench is the only word I can use, because the victims had been killed several days before, and this was the last of the feast.

"That night Doni himself told me the story of the bright visitor.

"After two or three days with the Wamuri people, giving three or four meetings each day, I said to Haru, 'How would you feel if I were to leave you to make this your base and to extend the work to other villages?'

"Haru was jubilant. 'I was hoping you would ask me to stay.'

"Six weeks later I was back in the Wamuri village and witnessed a marvelous transformation. They had built a new village. The old dubu was no longer used. Houses seemed to have sprung up everywhere, and a church was being built. As I sailed up to the village I found a line of about two hundred people standing side by side, dressed in new *lap laps* (loincloths).

"Haru said, 'I want you to shake hands with my people.' I shook hands and shook hands and shook hands.

"I asked Haru, 'How come all these new *lap laps?*' He said that he had selected twenty young men and had sent them by canoe to the mouth of the Turama and up another river to where there was a plantation. There they worked as long as it took to earn ten or twelve *lap laps* each. They then returned quickly to precede my return. Haru had not only organized the building of a new village and the purchase of new *lap laps* for everyone, but he himself had visited people in all the nearby villages and as a result of his preaching they, too, were there to meet me.

"As soon as I found a few minutes to spare I spoke to Doni. 'Your people should finish with their cannibalism,' I said.

" 'Master, we decided to end that the first night after you left. We have left that forever.'

" 'Well,' I said, 'what about the village people? Isn't it time they finished with their pigs?'

"Doni replied, 'There are no pigs left in this village. We killed them all. We won't even trade with them again.'

"This experience illustrates how the prayers of the boys and girls back at the mission station were being answered. Because Doni first saw the heavenly visitor at the time the students began their prayer bands, I feel my confidence in prayer—in their prayers—is justified.

"The whole story certainly put me on my knees. Doni was a man who, on his own admission, had never seen a white man before and had had no contact with any mission bodies. Yet he received a lesson in Bible health teachings, kept his first seventh-day Sabbath, and learned about tithing before we arrived. Do you wonder that the Master has a thousand ways of finishing the work that we know nothing about?"[2]

Some years later when the work was well established in the Turama River area, all cannibalism was gone. Further, the soul-liberating gospel message continues to spread in waves of power over the whole region.

One who had much personal communication with angels wrote, "When divine power is combined with human effort, the work will spread like fire in the stubble. God will employ agencies whose origin man will not be able to discern; angels will do a work which men might have had the blessing of accomplishing, had they not neglected the claims of God."[3]

1. From *Jewels From Green Hell* by Betty Buhler Cott (Review and Herald, 1969), pp. 173-179.
2. From *I Saw God's Hand* by E. L. Martin (Review and Herald, 1973), pp. 83-90.
3. Ellen G. White, *The Truth about Angels* (Pacific Press, 1996), pp. 267, 268.

# CHAPTER SEVEN

# Angels Who Rescue and Protect

$\mathcal{D}$esmond Doss, an American soldier hero whose name is familiar to many, was a medic during World War II. Doss fearlessly performed many rescue operations in the Pacific theater. His most amazing exploit involved the rescue of 75 wounded soldiers, lowering them over a steep cliff to safety while enemy bullets flew around him, sometimes coming so close he could feel them streaking by.

President Harry S. Truman decorated Desmond Doss with the Congressional Medal of Honor on the White House lawn for his unwavering valor in the face of extreme danger. But Doss would not have been around to rescue those 75 soldiers had he not been rescued himself several years before the war.

Desmond and his young nephew Gary were playing on a beach along the Atlantic coast. Gary's new beach ball somehow got away from him and began drifting out to sea. Though not a very good swimmer, Desmond could not refuse his little nephew's appeal for him to go out and retrieve the ball. Desmond swam through the

97

shallow water for a few hundred feet before he realized that the widening distance between himself and the ball was caused by a strongly ebbing tide.

A feeling of desperation washed over him. He knew it would be impossible to swim against the tide back to shore. If only he could catch up with the ball, then he could hold on to it as a kind of life preserver, but it was getting farther from him each moment. But Desmond was used to praying, so he offered up this simple plea: "Lord, help me!"

Desmond looked about. He could hardly be seen now from the receding shore, and the ball was now drifting from his sight. But then something else came into view—a small motorized fishing boat. The two men in the boat appeared to be pulling in fishing nets and preparing to go farther out in the ocean. Desmond prayed that they would notice him. He called out but realized that the boat's engine drowned out his voice.

Then the fishermen spotted the big beach ball coming their way. One of them bent over the side of the boat and retrieved the ball. Peering around, they also spotted Desmond and immediately came to his rescue. One of the men reached over the side of the boat and said, "Let me help you in."

Soon the boat drew close to shore. The other fisherman asked, "Can you make it from here?" The water was shallow, so, thanking the men, Desmond stepped out and waded ashore with his nephew's beach ball. On the beach he turned to wave at his rescuers, but there were no men, no boat, not even the wake of the boat's path through the sea. To this day, Desmond Doss believes that angels rescued him from drowning.

❦ ❦ ❦

Pastor Michael and his family served the Lord faithfully in central Africa. Through their beautiful Christian influence many people in the villages and countryside for miles around had accepted Christ. Then, in the 1970s, political trouble began to brew in that country. Armed guerrillas swarmed the area killing many people, pillaging hamlets and isolated homes, and spreading terror across that land. They were especially determined to kill all who had become "infected" with Christianity, "the white man's religion." But Pastor Michael knew that Christ is the Redeemer of all humanity, and that in His eyes, people of every nation, race, language, and tribe are welcomed into His family. While some of his compatriots were giving up Christianity in order to save their own lives, Pastor Michael continued to believe his Lord and visit his members, as well as conduct Bible studies among inquirers.

He learned that his activities had stirred the rage of the local revolutionaries, and that he was marked for death. Pastor Michael's faithful members warned him that his life was in great danger. But the good pastor thought, *If I flee, then my people will see Christianity as a coward's religion. How often I have taught my congregation that God is a mighty Protector; that the God Who was with Shadrach, Meshach, and Abednego in the fiery furnace, and with Daniel in the lion's den, is the same yesterday, today and forever. How often I have taught them to memorize promises such as "He who dwells in the secret place of the most High, shall abide under the shadow of the Almighty," and, "God is our refuge and strength, a very present help in trouble. Therefore we will not fear." I cannot leave. I must stay and minister to my flock, and support them in these days of trial and difficulty.*

One night, Pastor Michael returned home after spending a long day visiting and praying with his people, many of whom had retreated into hidden shelters amid the surrounding hills and woods for fear of harm from the revolutionaries. Moments after sitting down with his family for supper, the pastor heard angry, agitated voices approaching their hut. Soon their little dwelling, which was circular in shape and made of straw and thin wood, was surrounded.

The local guerrilla leader called out, "Pastor Michael! We know that you are in there. My men can see you through the window with your wife and three children. You are a traitor to your country and to the honor of your ancestors. We have tried you and sentenced you to die. We could shoot you, but that would be too easy a death for such a scoundrel as you. You will burn, and your God will not be able to do anything for you."

Then, turning to his soldiers, the captain of the band ordered, "Throw the torches all over the roof and on the sides of the hut. Don't let any of the occupants escape. Shoot only if they try to get out."

Immediately Pastor Michael and his family went to their knees and asked God for mercy and protection. The flames that now engulfed the house grew hotter and hotter, and smoke filled their little one-room shelter. Staying close to the floor, where the air was still somewhat breathable, they awaited the end. Yet all the while they continued to pray that God would spare them from pain and death, if that was His will. Then suddenly Pastor Michael saw a clearing through the smoke and a brightness that exceeded the surrounding flames. A luminous figure with a smiling face appeared through a hole in the side of the house, beyond which Pastor Michael could see the clear, cool evening sky.

This shining figure, accompanied by others like him, took Pastor Michael and his family out through the hole in the wall, while the flames continued to rage. This angelic rescue squad then bore the pastor and his family to the edge of the woods a mile or so distant. Telling the stunned pastor and his wife which way to go, the celestial deliverers quietly disappeared.

As the family stood in astonished silence, Pastor Michael could hear the commotion at his burning house. Following the angels' instruction, he and his family plunged into the trackless woods, feeling led safely all the way by invisible guides, who kept them from stumbling over rocks and roots or becoming entangled in the thick underbrush.

Months later, the leader of this band of destroyers, on learning the outcome of his evil work, sought out Pastor Michael and with his help accepted Christ as his Savior.

❦ ❦ ❦

Another angel rescue story sent into the office of the *Voice of*

*Prophecy* radio broadcast bears telling here. Karen L. of Anderson, California calls her story "Angel Hands."

"It was a beautiful afternoon in March 1984. We were living in Napa, California. My six children, my husband, and I were on a ride in our Chevy station wagon. We had driven over to the ocean and were headed back home, singing as we went. It had been a perfect day and the sun would soon be setting.

"As we cruised along a country road at about 40 mph, we saw a huge buck standing beside the road. It started to bound into the woods but suddenly turned back and came straight across the road. My husband slammed on the brakes, but we knew it was too late. The deer tried to jump over the hood but it didn't jump high enough. We knew that if we hit the buck, it would come through the windshield.

"Suddenly the deer was picked up and lifted over the car. It was high enough that on its undersides we could see the perfect imprints of two hands. It was as if everything went into slow motion. All of us in the car were able to see it. My husband, Bruce, stopped the car, and we all sat still for a bit, marveling at what we had just seen.

"That day will always be special to us, the day we saw the angel hands."

Again and again, the stories sent in by our Voice of Prophecy friends remind us that God's promise is dependable: "He shall give his angels charge over thee, to keep thee in all thy ways. They shall bear thee up in their hands" (Psalm 91:11, 12, KJV). Or, if necessary, they will bear up a deer to keep it from causing an accident.

❦ ❦ ❦

Angels are not only good bodyguards; they are also talented at guiding our footsteps into the paths of righteousness. They read character and warn us against being lured into evil company that would pollute our minds or bodies. God's promise is, "Behold, I send an Angel before you to keep you in the way and to bring you into the place which I have prepared" (Exodus 23:20).

Ultimately, that place is heaven, and all along the way, God wishes us to spiritually live in heavenly places through Christ Jesus (see Ephesians 2:6).

God knew a little girl who loved Jesus and needed His special protection in order to maintain her heaven-bound purity. Writing to us from Coquille, Oregon, Marie Johnson tells us about this little girl, a relative of hers from an earlier generation.

"Jessie was three years old when her mother took her to the lumber camp where Grandma and the aunties lived. Mama was expecting a new baby, and in the early days of the twentieth century it was customary to be with family at such a time.

"The camp was a rowdy place—rough men doing rough work, and wild teen-aged boy cousins running in a pack. It was daunting for a three-year old.

"One quiet summer afternoon Jessie was kneeling in the path in the middle of the camp, running her little cars on the roads she had carved in the dust. Glancing up, she saw her angel walk around the corner of the house and approach her. Jessie's mother had told her about angels, about *her* angel who always watched over her. Instinctively she recognized him as her own. He stopped beside her and held out his hand. Jessie rose to her feet, took his hand and walked with him down the path into the woods. The path led to the wreck of an old cabin. They approached it and the angel lifted Jessie up so she could see through the window.

"She could see herself inside the cabin, surrounded by her rough cousins. They were molesting her. 'Don't come here with those boys,' the angel instructed her. 'They will hurt you.' He lowered her to the ground, and the next thing Jessie knew, she was again running her little cars on their dusty roads.

"A few minutes later her cousins came roistering down the path. 'Hey, Jessie, come with us.'

" 'No.'

" 'Aw, c'mon, Jess. We got somethin' to show you.'

" 'No.'

" 'We got candy in the old cabin. Want some?'

" *'No!'* Jessie answered with such force that the boys glanced nervously about to see if an adult had heard. They slunk silently away, and those boys didn't bother Jessie again that summer.

"This experience became more precious to Jessie as she matured and realized how special it was. She cherished it in her heart, but she was a grown woman with children of her own before she mentioned it to a soul. One day she confided the experience to her mother.

" 'Oh, darling,' her mother replied. 'I was so worried about you that summer. I knew those were vile boys, and I begged God to protect you. How wonderfully He answered my prayers! And I'm glad that I had told you about your special angel so you recognized him when he came to you.' "

Angels linger where purity is sought, and where the love of Jesus is welcomed as life's ruling power.

❦ ❦ ❦

God's protection, though generally invisible, sometimes appears in dramatic and unexpected ways. At times evil men rise up with implacable hostility against God's servants, and He intervenes through His angels to work mighty deliverance. King David, reflecting on this kind of situation, prayed, "Let those be put to shame and brought to dishonor who seek after my life; let those be turned back and brought to confusion who plot my hurt. let them be like chaff before the wind, and let the angel of the Lord chase them" (Psalm 35:4, 5).

It is not advisable to reveal what part of Africa this next story comes from. Suffice it to say that it took place in an area where the preaching of the gospel was not welcome, and where the angel of the Lord provided protection that would be the envy of any trick photographer.

"Who will join me in a promise to go and kill the missionary Joe, and not to rest until it is done?" asked the ringleader of the opposition to the missionaries' presence in their region.

Seventeen voices shouted in approval, and these raging men

swore that they would kill Joe and his family. At once they set out to accomplish their task.

Joe knew nothing of this. He had gone off to work on a log he was preparing for a canoe. He had prayed that God would protect and guide in everything he should do that day. In his hand were an ax and other tools plus a small bag of stones for a sling he had made.

Suddenly he was confronted with seventeen angry men. "Put down your ax and talk to us," called the leader of the group.

Joe handed the ax to a friend nearby and walked toward the group. "Now!" came a yell. "Now! Kill him! Kill him!" Joe had time only to back up to a coconut palm when all seventeen fell on him, shouting that the government had ordered them to kill the missionaries. This was a lie, but Joe in his simplicity thought that if the government had deserted him, at least he ought to defend himself.

Joe says to this day that he was not conscious of hitting any-one. Those who looked on say that it seemed as if the men who attacked him fell down from only light blows. But at the end of the first charge, five of the attackers lay on the ground. The twelve who were left rallied to attack again.

A crowd had gathered. Seeing that it was an uneven fight, they held back the twelve men until Joe had recovered his breath. Once more the twelve rushed upon him. Again the miraculous happened, and another four men lay unconscious or out of action on the ground.

One of the eight men left, more determined than the others, drew a dagger and rushed at Joe. Seeing the dagger poised above him and waiting for the blow to fall, Joe thought only of his family and his work. "O Lord, deliver me!" he cried. He saw the rage in his attacker's face, and he saw the gleaming blade descend. He knew it was over for him. But suddenly the dagger was gone! It had gone! And a frightened, screaming man was running away with blood pouring from his hand. Somehow, and Joe cannot say how, the dagger was drawn backward out of the attacker's hand. Joe had been saved!

Frightened and jabbering among themselves, Joe's attackers retreated slowly to their canoe. They took the wounded man with them.

Joe made his way home to his wife, Rosi. When she saw him, bruised and covered with blood and dust, she was greatly disturbed. Soon, however, the blood was washed off; and as she heard the story of Joe's deliverance she was greatly encouraged.

"If God can deliver you from seventeen men, then surely He can keep us safe from other dangers."

Together they knelt and thanked God, sure now that whatever happened, God would be with them. Eventually, after much more persecution and ostracism, Joe and his family succeeded in bringing many of the superstition-bound people of that country to a saving knowledge of Christ. His deliverance from the seventeen men made a marked difference in the attitude of many in that region.

Only in heaven will we have a full picture of the numerous times angels have rescued us from danger. Many of us go through life without any noticeable evidence that this has been so. But when God opens our eyes to the reality of all that we experienced on earth, then we will see clearly that our angels averted disasters that could easily have ended our lives.

But now and then, their presence is made visible—often briefly, as we shall see from Jill Parchment's story of Douglas Warden, her father.

Douglas Warden was a very conservative Englishman. In fact, letters to him were addressed "F. Douglas Warden, Esquire." He was one of the chief executives in the Norwich Union Life Insurance Society, in their high-rise head office in downtown Calcutta, India.

Known for its burgeoning population of several million inhabitants in the early 1940s, Calcutta was a "City of Joy" for some and certainly a city of communal unrest for many others. Riots sparked as easily as striking a match. Quite often these were aimed at rival political or religious groups, and sometimes these groups merged to fight against the English "Imperialists" who claimed India as part of the British Empire.

On one such occasion Douglas was leaving his office after a long but successful day figuring insurance cases and premiums. His chauffeur drove him along the main thoroughfares until the congestion of rioters forced him off the road. Douglas decided to walk the remaining distance to his residence while the chauffeur drove the vehicle back to its rented garage.

Just under 6 feet, Douglas was a well-built man. He started off at an easy gait, striding along the outskirts of the crowds. Before he could get very far, however, his western apparel and looks drew the hostility of the mob. "Quit India, Englishman!" some roared as they grabbed him. Away sailed his western hat, like an airborne Frisbee. Next his striped tie was wrenched from his neck and flung down. Douglas remained calm and breathed a silent prayer to the Lord, with whom he had maintained daily devotional contact for many years.

Yet despite his plea to God, the mood of the rioters grew ugly and menacing. Douglas stood erect and even managed a friendly smile at his tormentors. Just as they were about to make a rush at him, a tall Indian of striking appearance called out *"Tiro! Tiro! (Wait! Wait!)."* From Hindi he switched into English.

"I know this Englishman. He is a good man. He helps our country, Mother India!" Making his way without opposition through the crowd, he put a long, muscled arm across Douglas's shoulders and, addressing him, he continued, *"Chulo, sahib* (Come along, sir). Let us go in this direction." His other arm, outstretched, opened a way through the rioters as the two walked on confidently till they reached a deserted area of the city.

"Continue down this street," he cautioned. "You will recognize your bearing and be close to your home." Douglas nodded affirmatively as he scanned the roads ahead and then turned to thank his rescuer, who could not have gone more than a few steps. But no one was in sight. Douglas knew then that an angel had rescued him from certain death.

Evidently the angels do not wish to be the special objects of our attention, for time and again, they disappear when their job is done. However, they continue to be with us, invisibly guiding and protecting. Their aim is always to draw our attention to the Savior, Jesus, who sent them on their mission.

❦ ❦ ❦ ❦

Pastor Moyo had just retired from more than thirty years of active service as a minister. He decided to return to his native village in the mountains of Zimbabwe. Fixing up his old family hut, he and his wife were soon comfortably situated. As a consecrated servant of God and faithful tithe-payer, Pastor Moyo was blessed with good health and a comfortable living. But a neighbor of his about the same age, whom we shall call Inclemento, quickly became jealous of Brother Moyo. He contrasted his own shabby circumstances with those of the retired pastor, whom he had known in his youth. He also despised Christianity as a poisonous European import.

So Inclemento decided to have Moyo killed. He did this by reporting him to the local military police substation in town, about eight miles away. Fabricating a tale about Moyo acting as a plotter for the overthrow of the government, Inclemento prompted the captain to send out a detachment of soldiers the next day to kill Moyo.

At the appointed time the soldiers appeared, and without any semblance of official inquiry began to beat Pastor Moyo with unrestrained fury. Considering his age and the force of their blows, they left him for dead at the roadside after several minutes of brutalizing treatment. Inclemento was satisfied, now that his "enemy" was out of the way.

Several days later, as he was passing by Moyo's hut to see how his widow was getting on, Inclemento saw, to his horror and astonishment, the pastor, bent over with bruises and other injuries, but still alive and moving around inside his hut. Moyo had no intention of seeking retaliation, but the Bible tells us that the wicked flee when no man is in pursuit. Fearing now for his own safety, Inclemento dashed off to the little military outpost in town and breathlessly panted out the story of Moyo's mysterious survival. "If he reports us," Inclemento said, "then we could all get into serious trouble with the government."

"Maybe so," replied the captain. "We'll come out right away and finish him off for good this time."

Hastening to Moyo's village with a detachment of twelve soldiers, the captain and his men cautiously approached the hut. There they saw Moyo feebly shuffling across his room and were about to raise their rifles to shoot him, when they heard low, sinister voices in a clump of trees a dozen yards or so from Moyo's house. The captain whispered to his men, "We can get Moyo later. He can't run. Let's investigate those voices."

Slowly they approached the trees, rifles poised for action. They heard what sounded like several men reviewing a plot to overthrow the government in low, urgent tones. In alarming detail these conspirators discussed implementing their plans in just a few days.

Motioning quietly to his men, the captain directed them to move in on these plotters and round them up. Slowly they approached the place from which the voices were coming. But as the soldiers advanced, the plotters moved off to a more distant part of the straggling grove that led away from Moyo's house to the outskirts of the village. Several times the soldiers attempted to surround the plotters in this manner, only to find that they had mysteriously eluded them. The conversation continued as though the plotters had no idea of being overheard.

Following these voices to the end of the grove, the soldiers were baffled as to why they could not close in on them or get a view of any of these insurrectionaries discussing their deadly intrigues.

The soldiers looked at one another as if to say, "What do we do now?" But then they heard the voices again, this time in a thick, isolated clump of trees about fifty feet away. *Now* the plotters were as good as captured. It was an easy matter for the soldiers to surround this small patch of woods. No one could escape from their circle. With guns at the ready, they closed in on the men, whose treacherous talk continued without interruption. In the center was a small clearing. There they heard rustling and discovered six grazing donkeys that looked up at their captors with momentary surprise and then nonchalantly went on munching leaves. Here were the plotters.

Ruefully looking at his men, the captain said, "Let's return to base, and leave Moyo alone. We shouldn't be bothering anyone with a God who protects him like this. There is no plot. We are fools, and Inclemento is a liar." [1]

❧ ❧ ❧ ❧

Our next two stories are intimately associated with the Voice of Prophecy. Roberta B. of Escondido, California writes:

"As a young married couple we lived in Phoenix, Arizona, where my husband was the church pastor. Jerry Pettis and his family lived at the other end of the state in Globe, where he was the pastor. Whenever possible we visited the Pettis family. This one weekend was special, because the Voice of Prophecy staff and the King's Heralds would be at Jerry's church.

"In the late 1930s most roads were two lanes wide. They were narrow but with much less traffic. On this particular weekend, we got started later than usual. It was dark as we entered a stretch where the hills reached high on our left and to our right down into a deep valley. A truck was following not far behind us, and we felt comforted to have someone else around in this area.

"As we rounded a curve, we saw a monstrous bull in the road. My husband put on the brakes and turned to the right, since the bull was heading for the hills to the left. We struck him a glancing blow—and instantly we were airborne.

"The truck driver behind us slammed on his brakes and stopped, jumped out, and ran down the mountain side.

"To our amazement, the car landed right side up, twenty feet down on a road in a small clearing. For moments we sat without

109

moving, not sure whether we were dead or alive. Then we saw a light behind us and heard the truck driver crashing through the bushes, carrying a light. My husband tried to get out but his door wouldn't open, so we all got out my door. The children were so frightened they hadn't said a word—but when the door opened they joyfully said, 'We're all right, Mommy!'

"The truck driver was joyous, too, and almost as frightened. He said he had seen an accident like this before and everyone was injured. To find our car right side up and all of us OK was a big surprise to him. He kept shaking his head and saying, 'It's a miracle!' We heartily agreed, and I told him, 'It was the hand of God!' His face lit up, and he repeated the words, nodding his head.

"With the aid of the flashlight my husband and the truck driver found a dirt road that ran along the ravine, parallel to the highway. Then, finding a connecting access road, we drove back with our helper to his truck. He just kept shaking his head and repeating the words, 'It had to be the hand of God!'

"We thanked the man with all our hearts, and then we bowed our heads and thanked God in prayer. We told him we were going to have a meeting in Globe the next day and that our friends from The Voice of Prophecy would be there. We felt sure everyone would rejoice in this miracle. He looked at us with shining eyes and said, "Could I come to the meeting?" We assured him of a hearty welcome.

"The truck driver did come to the meeting, and I never saw a happier man in my life. At the end of the service he stood and declared, 'I would like to belong to a church that is guided by *the hand of God!*' Shortly afterward he was baptized."

❦ ❦ ❦ ❦

H. M. S. Richards, founder of The Voice of Prophecy, tells of an amazing series of incidents that occurred in one of his father's evangelistic meetings many years ago.

"My father held a tent meeting, and I was his tentmaster that summer—my first time on the conference payroll. It was my responsibility to look after the tents. I lived in a small tent in back of the large tent. Almost impenetrable brush and weeds covered the lot behind my tent.

"Father's tent was pitched on a corner lot. On two sides stood large trees spaced quite closely together. On one side up near the tent was a little shoe-mending shop.

"On this particular night Father was preaching on 'The Great Red Dragon.' He always warned the people, 'I never preach on "The Great Red Dragon" without something happening. Something exciting takes place.' Of course, that helped to bring a bigger crowd.

"It was a hot August night. Father had asked me to put all the sides of the tent up so the air could come through. People were sitting on their front porches in the houses around. It was a sleepy night.

"Of course, nobody had automobiles in those days—only horse-drawn vehicles. Wagons, buggies, horses with saddles on them, all were tied up around the tent. I'd patrol around every little while to see that everything was all right while Father preached.

"He had almost come to the close of the sermon, and nothing unusual had occurred. I was outside checking things out. All the horses were standing around with their heads down. One big white horse, tied to a tree, was sound asleep.

"Suddenly, just as though someone had stuck a sword into him, that horse gave a snort and leaped right up in the air. He broke the rope that had fastened him to the tree, and started to plunge right toward the entryway of the tent. One more leap would have taken him right into the congregation.

"Father heard and saw this commotion and said, 'You're dismissed!' He did it so that people could run out, but it happened so fast that no one had time to move from their chairs.

"Just as the horse reached the entryway to the tent, he reared back and turned almost as though he were on a swivel, just as though some unseen guard were there. He ran off and got all tangled up in the brush behind the big tent and couldn't free himself.

"While this was happening, two horses on the other side of the tent broke loose and darted toward the entryway, trying to gallop into the tent with their buggy behind them. Again it happened very fast. Just as they got there they reared up and turned away. Kicking the buggy to pieces, they ran off into the brush and became tangled up.

"While this was going on another horse broke loose up the street, taking two or three boards off the side of the shoe shop along with a wagon wheel. He tried to get into the tent at that same place but turned away just as the others had done, also ending up in the brush. Everything happened so fast that the people were still sitting there in the tent when the commotion ceased. They'd had no time to move.

"The farmers had to come the next day and haul away the pieces of broken buggies and wagons. It was a very strange experience, something I'll never forget. I was supposed to be keeping order, but I couldn't do a thing. I'm convinced that only the angels guarding the tent saved the people from a serious accident." [2]

❦❦❦

The prince of circuit-riding preachers, John Wesley, with whom H. M. S. Richards's great-great grandfather rode in gospel service, tells an angel story from the year he turned seventy-two. Exciting though this story is, Wesley told it in characteristically calm, methodical fashion.

"Mon. May 20, 1774. About nine I set out for Horsley, with Mr. Hopper and Mr. Smith. I took Mrs. Smith and her two little girls in the chaise with me. About two miles from the town, just on the brow of the hill, on a sudden, both the horses set out, without any visible cause, and flew down the hill like an arrow out of a bow. In a minute John [the driver] fell off the coach-box. The horses then went on full speed, sometimes to the edge of the ditch on the right, sometimes on the left. A cart came up against them; they avoided it as exactly as if the man had been on the [driver's] box. A narrow bridge was at the foot of the hill; they went directly over the middle of it; they ran up the next hill with the same speed; many persons meeting us, but getting out of the way. Near to the top of the hill was a gate, which led into a farmer's yard. It stood open; they turned short, and ran through it without touching the gate on one side, or the post on the other. I thought, 'However, the gate which is on the other side of the yard, and is shut, will stop them.' But they rushed through it as if it had been a cobweb, and galloped on through the cornfield. The little girls cried, 'Grandpapa, save us.' I told them, 'Nothing will hurt you; do not be afraid;' feeling no more fear or care (blessed be God!) than if I had been sitting in my study. The horses ran on, till they came to the edge of a steep precipice. Just then Mr. Smith, who could not overtake us before, galloped in between. They stopped in a moment. Had they gone on ever so little, he and we must have gone down together.

"I am persuaded both evil and good angels had a large share in this transaction; how large we do not now know; but we shall know hereafter.

"I think some of the most remarkable circumstances were: 1. Both the horses, which were tame and quiet as could be, starting out in a moment just at the top of the hill, and running down full speed. 2. The coachman's being thrown on his head with such violence, and yet not hurt at all. 3. The chaise running again and again to the edge of each ditch, and yet not into it. 4. The avoiding the cart. 5. The keeping just the middle of the bridge. 6. The turning short through the first gate, in a manner that no coachman in England could have turned them, when in full gallop. 7. The going through the second gate as if it had been but smoke, without slackening their pace at all. This would have been impossible, had not the end of the chariot-pole struck exactly on the centre of the gate; whence the whole, by the sudden, impetuous shock, was broken into small pieces. 8. That the little girl, who used to have fits, on my saying, 'Nothing will hurt you,' ceased crying, and was quite composed. Lastly. That Mr. Smith struck in just then; in a minute more we had been down the precipice. And had not the horses then stopped at once, they must have carried him and us down together! 'Let those give thanks whom the Lord hath redeemed, and delivered from the hand of the enemy.' " [3]

What more can we say about the resourcefulness, vigilance, and agility of God's protecting angels, who encamp round about those who fear Him? Not until we are in heaven will we realize how actively they have intervened time and again for our protection. But let us never forget that beyond their physical protection of our lives, the angels are ceaselessly laboring to bring sinful, weak beings like us into a saving connection with God.

---

1. From Mike Pearson, pastor of Highland View Academy Seventh-day Adventist Church, Mt. Aetna, Maryland.
2. By H. M. S. Richards, Sr. as told in *H. M. S. Richards, A Biography* by Robert E. Edwards (Review and Herald, 1998), pp. 64, 65.
3. From the journal of John Wesley (no date).

# CHAPTER EIGHT

# Angels Who Sing

The Sabbath was drawing to a close as Luella Crane and her two children, Mira, 9 and Bob, 12, walked out of the back door of their home for sunset worship outdoors.

Their chairs stood at the back of the yard where the children had been playing during the week. Not too far away, behind this little nook, towering fir trees lifted their branches high above the mossy, fern-covered ground. That would be the perfect place for their devotions, Luella felt.

Generally, Luella's courage was good, but she had experienced overwhelming trials, trying to raise her small children alone since the tragic death of her husband some years before. This had been an especially trying week, and she found herself feeling discouraged.

As the three stepped outside, an unusual sky caught their attention with its rich golden hues filtering through the trees. Luella felt she had never seen such a brilliant yellow sky. The children noticed too, pausing with their mother to admire its breathtaking beauty.

Then the sound of music drifted down to them from the upper branches of those majestic trees. Softly it began with the sound of harps. Gradually it swelled into a rich symphonic orchestra. Then came the voices of singing—and such singing! Luella stood transfixed; it was the loveliest music she had ever heard!

Mira was frightened. Plainly, it was not a human orchestra and choir sounding from the treetops. And no one was visible as they looked up. Mira started to cry as she stood between her mother and her brother, Bob.

Luella slipped a comforting arm about her daughter, and Bob also reached an arm about his little sister. Then Luella spoke. "We must surely be hearing angels sing." It just had to be. As they listened in awestruck wonder, these words drifted down to them:

"Oh, Shepherd divine, I know Thou art mine: Thy search through the night was for me. This bleak world is cold, but warm is Thy fold. My Shepherd, I follow Thee."

The last golden notes faded into silence except for the voice of a night bird as the evening shadows fell. Returning to the house, Luella went at once to her piano. Her fingers flew across the keys as she attempted to recapture the melody they had just heard. Mira told me that her mother played it again and again.

Only a few years later, Herbert Work, a composer and music teacher, wrote both the words and music to this same song the angels had sung that Sabbath evening to Luella and her children. Among the many songs he had written, it seemed to Herbert Work that this one was his best.

At the time Herbert Work wrote this song he had not so much as heard of Luella or her experience. He told me his inspiration for songs always seemed to come to him when he was in the woods. He was behind the barn at Pacific Union College, among the trees, when the inspiration came to him to write "My Shepherd." It was just a quiet inspiration, nothing as dramatic as Luella and her children had encountered. But the music and the words were identical to those Luella and her children had heard several years earlier.[1]

❦ ❦ ❦ ❦

Years before this, a special messenger of the Lord, Ellen White, had the privilege of hearing angels sing. She recorded the following from a vision she had in her youth.

> Then I was pointed to the glory of heaven, to the treasure laid up for the faithful. Everything was lovely and glorious. The angels would sing a lovely song, then they would cease singing and take their crowns from their heads and cast them glittering at the feet of the lovely Jesus, and with melodious voices cry, 'Glory, Alleluia!' I joined with them in their songs of praise and honor to the Lamb, and every time I opened my mouth to praise Him, I felt an unutterable sense of the glory that surrounded me. Said the angel, 'The little remnant who love God and keep His commandments and are faithful to the end will enjoy this glory and ever be in the presence of Jesus and sing with the holy angels.'[2]

This vision is corroborated by the book of Revelation's frequent references to future glory in the heavenly kingdom, when redeemed people and angels will blend their voices together in singing praise to God (see Revelation 4:6-11; 5:8-14; 7:10-12).

We can be sure that the singing up in heaven will not be tainted by evil influences but will have a sacred sublimeness in keeping with the glory and purity of God's character. Writing again about what she heard in heaven, Ellen White wrote,

> I have been shown the order, the perfect order, of heaven, and have been enraptured as I listened to the perfect music there. After coming out of vision, the singing here has sounded very harsh and discordant. I have seen companies of angels, who stood in a hollow square, every one having a harp of gold. . . . There is one angel who always leads, who

first touches the harp and strikes the note, then all join in the rich, perfect music of heaven. It cannot be described. It is melody, heavenly, divine, while from every countenance beams the image of Jesus, shining with glory unspeakable.[3]

A group of faithful believers in Surabaya experienced a fore-taste of the joy of hearing angels sing in heaven. Their experience occurred in the midst of a deadly bombing campaign during World War II. Arthur Maxwell, veteran storyteller, narrates their experience:

*"Bang! Boom! Bang! Boom! Boom!* The bombs were dropping all around. Buildings were burning and falling. People were screaming and crying. Already most of the city of Surabaya had been destroyed in the terrible bombardment. Thousands of men, women, and children had been killed.

"Almost all the churches had been bombed, all except the little Adventist church, where Christian and Ketty, with their father and mother and some friends, were talking together, wondering how long their lives would be spared, and whether it would be their turn next to die.

"As the bursting bombs came ever nearer and nearer, they could see, through the windows, great fires blazing all about them. Father, who was the minister of the church, then urged them all to take refuge in the baptismal tank. It was not much of an air-raid shelter, but the best they had.

"This tank, which was behind the pulpit, was not very large or deep, but they all crowded into it. Then they began to pray.

"What a prayer meeting that was! Father prayed, and Mother, and then the children. Christian, just twelve years old, remembered the thirty-fourth psalm, especially where it says, 'The angel of the Lord encampeth round about them that fear him, and delivereth them.'

"Over and over again he pleaded, 'Send the angels, Lord, to encamp round about us and deliver us. Send the angels, Lord! Send the angels!'

"Then little Ketty, who was only four, began to plead: 'Dear Jesus, Thou hast promised to send Thine angels. Keep Thy promise. Oh, Jesus, send the angels!'

"So they prayed. And God in heaven heard.

"What happened next may seem to some unbelievable, but it really happened. I know this minister well. He is one of God's noblest servants, and he told me the story himself.

"As they prayed, the planes passed over, and the bombs fell farther and farther away. When the sky seemed clear again, Father went out into the church to see if all was well. It was. Not a spark of fire had fallen on the building. As he stood there, thanking God for His goodness, there came a loud knocking on the door. Going to see who it could be at such a time, he found two policemen there, with many angry civilians behind them.

" 'Who was singing in this church just now?' they demanded.

" 'Singing?' he said. 'Singing? Nobody. The church has been empty.'

" 'You're not telling the truth,' they said. 'We heard the singing, and we want to know what you mean by singing in here when the city is burning, and people are dying all around you.'

" 'Come in and see for yourself,' said Father.

"They came, and found the place empty, and went away wondering. Father also wondered. What could the police mean by saying that there had been singing in the church? He had not heard any.

"Then the bombers returned. Again the dreadful hum of their engines became louder and louder. Once more the bombs began to fall. So Father hurried back to the baptismal tank and told the others the strange story the police had told him. Then they prayed again. Once more, as the noise and terror of it all mounted about them, Christian and Ketty lifted up their voices to God, saying, 'Send the angels! Send the angels, Jesus! Keep Your promise! Send the angels!'

"And then they heard it too, that strange, sweet sound. Above the din of destruction, above the bombing and the burning, they heard the sound of singing. Beautiful singing, such as they had never heard before. And it was coming from the church, just as the police had said.

"And the song? It sounded, so he told me, just like the old, familiar hymn:

"All the way my Saviour leads me;
What have I to ask beside?
Can I doubt His tender mercy,
Who through life has been my guide?
Heavenly peace, divinest comfort,
Here by faith in Him to dwell!
For I know whate'er befall me,
Jesus doeth all things well.

"When the bombers had passed, all hurried out of the baptismal tank into the church. They found the building empty, without a sign that anyone had been there. Then again there came the loud knocking at the door, as police and people came to find out what it all meant. When, once more, they found nobody there save this handful of adults and children, they were amazed and could not believe their eyes.

"But Father understood now. So did Christian and Ketty. They knew their prayers had been answered. They knew that God had sent His angels to protect them, and they—O joy, O wonder of wonders—they had heard them singing!

"Today that Adventist church still stands in Surabaya, a monument to God's protecting power over His people in time of trouble, a testimony that the angels of the Lord still encamp round about them that fear Him, to deliver them." [4]

❦ ❦ ❦ ❦

King David declared, "You are my hiding place; you shall preserve me from trouble; you shall surround me with songs of deliverance" (Psalm 32:7). And God's angel choir brings those songs to us! What love our Redeemer has for us, and what value He places on our lives!

The next story is not only a beautiful example of music in the ministry of angels, but it also provides an unusual glimpse into the conflict between good and evil angels, a conflict that rages over every person who commits their life to Christ.

In 1994 three Christians went to live and work among the people on Hilantagaan, a tiny island that lies off the northern tip of the island of Cebu in central Philippines. Most of the islanders follow a religion that reveres a Filipino hero whom, they believe, was the reincarnation of Christ. Many of their beliefs mix elements of Christianity with occult practices. The Christians made friends, held Vacation Bible Schools, and shared their faith. Gradually, the people of the island began to open their hearts to these three lay workers. Some listened to their words of faith, and within a year, eight people were baptized.

The lay workers and the new believers laid plans to hold a series of evangelistic meetings on the island. They asked the *barangay* (village) captain for permission to hold the meetings in the open-air plaza at the center of the largest village on the island. The *barangay* captain had a Christian relative, so he willingly gave permission.

But when the devil saw the progress Christians were making in his territory, he was angry. He tried all sorts of tricks to disrupt the meetings. On the day that the meetings were to begin, the speaker suddenly became ill and was taken to the hospital. That evening a layman stepped in and spoke. Suddenly the sound system went dead. The speaker continued with his presentation while the soundman searched for the problem in the equipment. He found a wire that had been yanked loose in the amplifier and quickly repaired it. But within a few minutes the system went dead again. The soundman found that *the same wire* had been pulled loose. Again he repaired the wire, but this time he stood nearby to be sure no one tampered with the amplifier. But within a few minutes the same wire was torn out again.

Realizing that no human hand had torn the wire out, a group of believers began praying that God would restrain Satan's hand and prevent him from disrupting the meetings. The rest of the evening the amplifier wires were not touched.

The next evening the devil again tore out the wire. But when the prayer band began praying, the devil's mischief ended. The believers realized that prayer was their only defense against demonic sabotage. But the members of the prayer group wanted to hear the speaker's message, so they stopped praying. Immediately, the devil returned to cause mischief. The prayer band realized that they had to continue praying or the devil would create havoc.

Many other strange things happened to plague the little band of workers. These supernatural manifestations did not seem to surprise the people of this island. They knew that evil spirits were causing these disturbances and even suggested that if the Christians appeased the spirits, they would stop their mischief! Instead the believers prayed that God would show the people who was more powerful. The answer that came to encourage the band of harassed workers was most unusual.

The Filipino people enjoy the lovely custom of serenading. Very early in the morning, while it is still dark, friends gather under the window of the persons they wish to honor and will sing songs for them. The Christian believers on this island decided to form two serenading bands. They awoke about 3:00 A.M. each morning to serenade the islanders who were attending the meetings. The singing would awaken the people inside, who would then welcome the singers into the home for a brief visit, which always ended with prayer.

The believers tried to serenade several homes each day before dawn. But by the eighth night the group was simply too tired to wake up at 3:00 A.M. Suddenly the believers were awakened by the sound of beautiful singing. They hurried to the door and looked outside, but they could not see anyone. They dressed quickly and hurried toward the home of the other group of serenaders. On their way, they met the second group in the street. "Were you serenading us tonight?" they asked.

"No," the second group said. "You were serenading us!"

"No," the first group answered. "We overslept, and were awakened by beautiful singing! Was it not you?" All the believers had overslept, yet both groups had been serenaded. A hush fell over them as they realized that heavenly singers had serenaded them. With tears in their eyes, they hugged one another, grateful for the knowledge that God had blessed their efforts by sending His heavenly choir of angels to serenade and encourage them.

As the meetings ended, 18 new believers were baptized. A second group soon joined them, and today some 70 members meet in a lovely little church that they built on their island. They have forsaken the superstitions that held them in bondage to Satan, and they continue to share their faith in the God who is stronger than the devil. [5]

These stories help us see how Christian song is a vital channel of communication and faith building, and sometimes even of instruction. That is why Paul said, "Let the word of Christ dwell in you richly in all wisdom, teaching and admonishing one another in psalms and hymns and spiritual songs, singing with grace in your hearts to the Lord" (Colossians 3:16).

❦ ❦ ❦ ❦

Howard P. of Burnsville, North Carolina sent this thought-provoking angel story to the Voice of Prophecy office. It illustrates the soul-nurturing influence of godly music.

Ten-year-old Howard was sitting in church. It was an evening vespers meeting designed for the young people of the church. The little children were gathered on the front row, and most of the parents sat in the back. But the children Howard's age were scattered through the middle section. Howard was sitting alone this particular evening, with no one near him on either side or in front or back of him. A song service was in progress, but Howard was off in another world, daydreaming, as usual.

Howard's parents were careful to give him a Christian upbringing that included not only church attendance every week, but also church school. Still, Howard was not deeply interested in religious activities. As he sat there that evening oblivious to the voices of worship around him, something happened that grabbed his attention. Suddenly he heard a loud whisper in his left ear. *"Sing!"* the voice commanded. Howard whirled around to the left and then to the right, expecting to see someone who had spoken, but no one was anywhere near him. Astonished, he looked under the seat and found no one there. Yet the command had been so loud, so emphatic, and so unexpected that he knew he had not imagined it. It had to have been an angel. A bit shaken, Howard decided it was best to obey, so he started to sing.

Four years later Howard was baptized in the same church. And now, nearly 60 years later, he has shared this story. "I truly enjoy singing now," Howard says, "especially songs like 'Hiding in Thee' and 'How Great Thou Art.' And I have no doubt who spoke to me that evening."

As a power to bind us to God and dispel evil, Christian song stands in almost equal company with prayer. Songs are often deep prayers of the heart set to melody. Only in heaven will we fully understand how often the songs of faith, sung in the nighttime of our loneliness and sorrow, were a means of protecting us from the assaults of the enemy, in the realms of the seen and the unseen. Occasionally we may get a glimpse of this while on earth.

A striking instance of this protection comes from post–Civil War days in Mid-Atlantic America.

"It was Christmas Eve, 1875. Ira D. Sankey was traveling by steamboat up the Delaware River. It was a calm, starlit evening, and there were many passengers gathered on deck. Mr. Sankey was asked to sing. He stood leaning against one of the great funnels of the boat, and his eyes were raised to the starry heavens in quiet prayer. It was his intention to sing a Christmas song, but he was driven almost against his will to sing, 'Saviour, Like a Shepherd Lead Us.'

"Words and melody, welling forth from the singer's soul, floated out over the deck and into the deep stillness of the night. Every heart was touched.

124

"After the song was ended, a man with a rough, weather-beaten face came up to Mr. Sankey and said, 'Did you ever serve in the Union army?'

" 'Yes,' answered Mr. Sankey, 'in the spring of 1862.'

" 'Can you remember if you were doing picket duty on a bright, moonlit night in 1862?'

" 'Yes,' answered Mr. Sankey, very much surprised.

" 'So did I,' said the stranger, 'but I was serving in the Confederate army. When I saw you standing at your post I said to myself, 'That fellow will never get away from here alive.' I raised my musket and took aim. I was standing in the shadow, completely concealed, while the full light of the moon was falling upon you. At that instant, just as a moment ago, you raised your eyes to heaven and began to sing. Music, especially song, has always had a wonderful power over me: and I took my finger off the trigger.

" 'Let him sing his song to the end,' I said to myself. 'I can shoot him afterwards. He's my victim at all events, and my bullet cannot miss him.' But the song you sang then was the one you sang just now. I heard the words perfectly:

*We are Thine, do Thou befriend us,*
*Be the guardian of our way.*

" 'When you had finished your song it was impossible for me to take aim at you again. I thought, 'The Lord, who is able to save that man from certain death, must surely be great and mighty,' and my arm of its own accord dropped limp at my side.

" 'Since that time I have wandered about, far and wide, but when I just now saw you standing there praying as on that other occasion, I recognized you. Then your song wounded my heart. Now I ask that you help me find a cure for my sick soul.'

"Deeply moved, Mr. Sankey threw his arms about the man who in the days of the war had been his enemy. And that night the stranger found the Good Shepherd as his Saviour." [6]

Our privilege of working with angels for the salvation of others through song brings to life the words of the ancient prophet:

"How beautiful upon the mountains are the feet of the messenger who announces peace, who brings good news, who announces salvation, who says to Zion, 'Your God reigns.' Listen! Your sentinels lift up their voices, together they sing for joy" (Isaiah 52:7, 8, NRSV). Yes, they will sing together with angels to gather the ransomed of the Lord from near and far, that we may all join in chorus to sing His praises forever.

---

1. Adapted from Ida Mae Morley's article, "The Song," published in the North Pacific Union Conference *Gleaner*, May 5, 1990.
2. *Early Writings* (Review and Herald, 1945), p. 66.
3. *Evangelism* (Review and Herald, 1946), pp. 505, 506.
4. Arthur S. Maxwell, *The Children's Hour with Uncle Arthur* (Pacific Press, 1947), book 2, pp. 37-40.
5. Supplied by Charlotte Ishkanian, Silver Spring, Maryland.
6. Quoted with adaptations from Mrs. Charles E. Cowman, *Streams In the Desert*, vol. 2, reading for December 24.

# CHAPTER NINE

# *Angels Who Watch and Warn*

*C*laudia tossed and turned in her perfumed bed. It was not the crisp chill of the early spring morning that disturbed her slumbers, but a dream. This was no chaotic, macabre nightmare, but rather a vision of transcendent solemnity that flashed into the chambers of her soul with compelling urgency. Claudia did not have the imagination or depth of mind to create this dream from her inner self. An angel from heaven beamed the vision into her mind. Her husband, the governor, attending an emergency trial, needed to hear about this without delay. For Claudia's dream pertained to the man who stood on trial that very moment.

Springing from her bed, she swiftly but legibly wrote the words, "Have nothing to do with that righteous Man; for last night I suffered greatly in a dream because of Him."[1] What did the angel show Claudia in her dream that so distressed her?

One religious writer describes it this way:

Even now Pilate was not left to act blindly. A message from God warned him from the deed he was about to commit. In answer to Christ's prayer, the wife of Pilate had been visited by an angel from heaven, and in a dream she had beheld the Saviour and conversed with Him. Pilate's wife was not a Jew, but as she looked upon Jesus in her dream, she had no doubt of His character or mission. She knew Him to be the Prince of God. She saw Him on trial in the judgment hall. She saw the hands tightly bound as the hands of a criminal. She saw Herod and his soldiers doing their dreadful work. She heard the priests and rulers, filled with envy and malice, madly accusing. She heard the words, 'We have a law, and by our law He ought to die.' She saw Pilate give Jesus to the scourging, after he had declared, 'I find no fault in Him.' She heard the condemnation pronounced by Pilate, and saw him give Christ up to His murderers. She saw the cross uplifted on Calvary. She saw the earth wrapped in darkness, and heard the mysterious cry, 'It is finished.' Still another scene met her gaze. She saw Christ seated upon the great white cloud, while the earth reeled in space, and His murderers fled from the presence of His glory. With a cry of horror she awoke, and at once wrote to Pilate words of warning.[2]

How often God's watchers and holy ones have tried to intervene and turn the current of human thoughts heavenward. Pilate need not have been an agent in Christ's suffering. His could have been a shining example of manly resistance to the Sanhedrin's brutal hatred for Christ. He could have exercised judicial fortitude and honor, but like most men he crumbled under the pressure when the pressure was great. In every age true moral courage is rare, but when it is exhibited, how radiant a jewel it is!

More than anything, Pilate wanted to hold on to his governorship. He could not sacrifice worldly honor for the sake of justice and truth. But his self-serving spirit gained him no lasting advantage. Soon after Christ's crucifixion Pilate lost his governorship in disgrace, and died by his own hand. He could have avoided all that sorrow and ultimate loss in his life. If only he had listened to the warning.

Let's look at some stories of those who did heed the warning and were blessed beyond all expectation. Elizabeth M. was only 14 when she sent us this story:

"In 1993, I was 9 years old and my sister, Ruth, was ten. One day my mother went to pick up some literature at the Quiet Hour office, and Ruth and I were home alone. After a while we got into an argument—I don't recall what our squabble was about. I stormed upstairs to the loft overlooking the family room. Our family room had a cathedral ceiling and a stairway leading into a loft that we used as a classroom for our home school.

"Feeling bad about our fight, I sat at my study desk wanting to tell my sister that I was sorry and that I loved her. I thought about writing her a card. While pondering these thoughts, I also wondered if I was really sincere about my feelings. Heavy-hearted, I slowly began to make my way downstairs.

"I saw an angel on the landing where the steps turn to the right. He was very tall, maybe about 9 or 10 feet. I cannot adequately describe the angel's appearance. It was too beautiful for ordinary words. He was bright and was surrounded by a shimmering light of transparent gold. In his left hand he held a sword pointed downwards. His countenance held an expression of displeasure. Not displeasure as we think of it. Not anger. I sensed his deep concern for my well being and the decisions I would make. His goodness and love for me shone through, but still, feeling unfit to be in his presence, I couldn't help being scared.

"With a wave of his sword, the angel motioned for me to go down. He seemed to know the choice I was about to make. Then he disappeared, and I ran quickly down the stairs, scraping my right arm against the railing. I dashed into my parents' room, and my sister entered a few moments later. Immediately noticing my injured arm, she asked me what had happened. I was too overwhelmed to tell her the story, but ran into the living room and hid behind a chair. My sister suggested that we go for a walk. During our walk I was able to tell her in little spurts what had happened. We both cried and told each other how sorry we were as we held each other tightly."

At the Voice of Prophecy office we found Elizabeth's experience so interesting that we called her to ask how it has affected her life since that time. Elizabeth answered, "Following this experience with the angel there was a lot more peace between my sister and me. We both decided to work out our disagreements more kindly. I can't truthfully say that I've always been successful in this effort. But even now, more than five years later, I find it much easier to remember that Jesus really does want me to be good, and to reach out to Him for His love to be in my heart.

"Also, when I have conflicts with anyone, I try to work things out peaceably, and not to react too quickly. I try to make peace, even when I'm not at fault. Not that I wish to pretend I'm perfect. I have my faults and struggles. But I also know I have God's help to overcome and to become more and more like Jesus, who sent the angel to alert me to my serious temper problem and help me throughout life to gain the victory."

Elizabeth's amazing account of her angel experience calls to mind Jesus' beatitude: "Blessed are the peacemakers, for they shall be called sons of God" (Matthew 5:9). Paul exhorted believers, "Follow peace with all men, and holiness, without which no man shall see the Lord: looking diligently lest any man fail of the grace of God; lest any root of bitterness springing up trouble you, and thereby many be defiled" (Hebrews 12:14, KJV).

Recognizing that Elizabeth had humbly tried to learn the lesson her angel taught her, we asked her if she had experienced any other encounters with her angel. She replied, "Nothing quite so dramatic as that first one I wrote to you about. But I am now much more aware of God's closeness in my life, and often think of my angel's compassionate concern for me, and his guiding presence. I think for example of a recent time when I was scheduled to play my cello for special music at church. I was very nervous, afraid that I was going to botch it in front of the congregation. I was standing in our yard at home worrying about this when I felt my angel folding his arms around me and assuring me that it was going to come out right. Feeling at peace, I just practiced and prayed and asked God to help me play to His glory instead of mine. Everything did go OK after all when I played that Sabbath at church. I am very thankful for my angel. I wouldn't want to resist God by rejecting any part of this angel's ministry, because I know he comes to carry out God's will and guide me into all truth."

The Lord promised Israel, "I am going to send an angel in front of you, to guard you on the way, and to bring you to the place that I have prepared. Be attentive to him and listen to His voice; do not rebel against him, . . . for my name is in him" (Exodus 23:20, 21, RSV). In heaven we will fully understand how lovingly active and alert the angels have been to keep us in all our ways (see Psalm 91:11).

🕊 🕊 🕊 🕊

Gaston Paulin, a French Canadian who pastors a church in Tennessee, tells of a memorable incident in his childhood that illustrates the importance of listening to our angel when he prompts us with a message of warning. Gaston writes:

"In my childhood home we had a copy of a large painting that depicted a guardian angel tenderly watching over a sleeping baby. My belief in angels was as constant as the presence of the beautiful picture in the wall. But not until one fateful winter morning did I believe that my angel was always present to protect and guide me. It happened in my hometown of Quebec when I was 10 or 11 years old.

"A few weeks before, I had received a bright red toy shovel as a Christmas present. Eager for the opportunity to use it, I waited for snow. Every day after Christmas I sprang out of bed and ran to the window to see if it had snowed. Finally one night it came. Throughout the night big fluffy flakes had blanketed the stark landscape, transforming it into a world of pure and dazzling white. In the morning, after gazing out the window wide-eyed for a few moments, I raced downstairs to our living room, where the shovel lay waiting for us under the Christmas tree. I grabbed my shovel and, though still in my pajamas, started to put on my snow boots. My mother stopped me and insisted that I have breakfast and get fully dressed before rushing out to play. Never did a boy so hastily gulp down his food or put on his winter wear.

"Soon I was outside and reveling in the snow. A huge plowing tractor that passed along our street earlier left a high bank of snow in front of our driveway. It was perfect for digging a tunnel. Feverishly I set to work with my red shovel and soon hollowed out a space into which I could walk. It was so quiet and still inside my hand-dug cave, and I was so tired from all the exertion that without thinking about it I curled up, clutching my shovel, and fell asleep in my snug little retreat.

"Totally oblivious to where I was, I began to dream. But breaking in on my heavy slumbers I heard a voice urgently say, 'Gaston, wake up and get out.' Startled at first, I looked around but could see no one and hear nothing. Vaguely aware that I was still in my snow cave. I drifted off to sleep again. I do not know how many minutes passed before I heard the voice again, only this time more urgent and imperative, 'Gaston, wake up, and get out, *now!*'

"The voice awakened me like an electric shock. Forgetting everything else, I quickly scurried out of my little grotto. Moments later I saw a huge ice-grinding vehicle and dump truck move parallel up our street. The grinder was rapidly consuming the snow-bank, funneling it into the truck.

"Then it struck me—no one in my house or on the street knew where I had been. The voice must have been that of my angel. If he had not jarred me awake by his urgent command I would have been ground up with the snow and would have sprung awake too late to escape this gruesome end. How thankful I was for my angel who kept watch over me while I slept, and alerted me to my danger at the crucial moment.

"Ever since then have I never doubted the reality of guardian angels. This incident occurred more than 40 years ago, but throughout my life I have been positively affected by this experience. I have tried to make it a practice to seek God's guidance in all my activities, so that I might live to His glory. I look forward to thanking my angel face to face someday for his loving vigilance over me, and learning from him the innumerable other circumstances where he protected and guided me in harmony with my Saviour's will and purpose of my life."

❦ ❦ ❦ ❦

Peter Marshall, famous chaplain of the United States Senate in the late 1940s, left the world a rich legacy in his books of sermons and prayers. A special angel experience that took place when Peter was about 17 made it possible for him to live and bless the world with his ministry.

In his youth, Peter Marshall spent the summer working in the English village of Bamburgh, just south of the Scottish border. One night while walking back to Bamburgh from a nearby village, he decided to take a shortcut across the heath. He knew that there was an abandoned quarry in the area but was sure he could avoid it. It was a dark, overcast night, and the wind moaned cheerlessly over the stark landscape.

Suddenly an urgent, commanding tone called out his name, "Peter!"

Stopping, he asked, "Yes, who is it? What do you want?"

Hearing no reply, he supposed that he had imagined it from the sound of the wind. Walking on several paces more, he stopped again when the voice said with even greater urgency, "Peter!"

This time Peter stood still, attempting to peer through the impenetrable darkness. Shifting his position slightly, he stumbled and fell to his knees. Cautiously reaching out before him to search over the ground, he found nothing there. In a semicircle just before him was nothing but emptiness. He was standing on the brink of the quarry, a sheer cliff of terrifying height. No one could have survived a fall over the edge of that precipice.

From that time onward, Peter resolved to be obedient to that voice, which he knew was sent by God. Surely it was the voice of Peter's guardian angel, commissioned "to keep him in all his ways, and bear him up in his wings lest he dash his foot against a stone."

Wouldn't it make sense for all of us to ask God to keep us very sensitive to the voice of His Spirit and His angels, so that He can guide us through life according to His ideal plan? If we tapped into this high privilege, think of how many calamities we might avoid, and how many blessings we might gain. This is God's promise to us in His word: "And though the Lord gives you the bread of adversity and the water of affliction, yet your teachers will not be moved into a corner anymore, but your eyes shall see your teachers. Your ears shall hear a word behind you, saying, 'This is the way, walk in it,' whenever you turn to the right hand or whenever you turn to the left'" (Isaiah 30:20, 21). Jesus Himself said, " 'Everyone who is of the truth hears My voice'" (John 18:37). He spoke these beautiful words to Pilate while under hasty judicial examination. What a pity that Pilate didn't listen. How gloriously different would have been his own future if he had listened. And how wondrously different will be your future and mine if we follow God's voice.

---

1. Matthew 27:19, NASB.
2. Ellen G. White, *The Desire of Ages* (Pacific Press, 1940), p. 732.

# CHAPTER TEN

# *Angels of Justice*

*A*s we have seen repeatedly, the miraculous intervention of angels has not been limited to Bible times. And one of the angels' main functions is to operate as ministers of God's justice. After all, they delight in upholding God's righteous law. That is why the Psalmist declared, "Bless the Lord, ye his angels, that excel in strength, that do his commandments, hearkening unto the voice of his word" (Psalm 103:20, KJV). They love to vindicate the innocent, and often intervene in mysterious, unexpected ways.

When H. M. S. Richards's father, H. M. J. Richards, was a young boy in Exeter, England, he witnessed a remarkable event that impressed itself on the public mind for many years. Robert E. Edwards tells the story.

A young man named John Lee was accused and convicted of murder. Though he persistently maintained his innocence, he was sentenced to hang.

The night before his execution, young John Lee had a dream. He saw himself being led out of his cell and through the prison corridor to the gallows. There he ascended the thirteen steps to the platform. A guard blindfolded him and placed the noose around his neck. After Lee said his last words, the executioner pulled the lever to spring the trap door, but nothing happened. Then John Lee woke up.

The following morning, young H. M. J. Richards joined with most of Exeter's population as they stood around the prison, waiting to see the flag go up in the prison courtyard at the appointed moment to signal the accomplishment of the execution. They waited in vain, for the flag never appeared. John Lee's dream had proven true. It all went just as he had seen in his sleep. The trap door refused to function.

After their unsuccessful attempt, the guards led the prisoner from the scaffold, then carefully checked and oiled the simple machinery that operated the trap door. Placing a bag of sand on the trap door, they pulled the lever, and saw the bag drop to the pavement below. Again they placed Lee over the trap door, adjusted the noose over his neck, and pulled the lever with decisive force. But the trap stayed firmly locked in place.

With grim consternation the guards conducted Lee off the platform again and retested their equipment, only to find it in perfect working order. For the third time they led their submissive prisoner to the place of his scheduled execution. Making sure that the noose was snug and that he stood squarely on the middle of the trap door, they jerked the lever again. But the gallows refused to drop Lee to his judicially ordered death.

Shaken by this turn of events, the warden telegraphed Queen Victoria with the baffling news. She ordered Lee's sentence to be commuted to life imprisonment, since they had not been able to execute him after three tries. Years later, the authorities freed John Lee when someone finally confessed to the crime for which Lee had been unjustly condemned.

Who held up the trap door that was supposed to hurtle Lee to his dreadful end? Surely it was an angel, sent by the Lord to protect an innocent man.

Jesus, the ultimate innocent Man, refused to summon an angel guard when He was being subjected to injustice. His disciple Peter erupted with indignation at the moment of Jesus' arrest, however. Peter unsheathed his sword and swung out wildly, and he succeeded in severing the ear of Malchus, the servant of Israel's high priest. Lightly freeing his hands from His captors, Jesus reached out and healed Malchus's wounded ear and, turning to Peter, said, " 'Put your sword back into its place, for all who take the sword will perish by the sword. Or do you think that I cannot now pray to My Father, and He will provide Me with more than twelve legions of angels? How then could the Scriptures be fulfilled that it must happen thus?' " (Matthew 26:52-54). By His very statement that He could have called legions of angels to His side at that fateful hour, Jesus was bringing to our attention how closely angels monitor affairs on earth, and how keenly they are poised to uphold justice.

❦ ❦ ❦ ❦

James and Ellen White were newlyweds when they conducted an evangelistic series in a small New England town in 1847. At first, some of the townspeople ridiculed the idea of this young couple attempting to do the work that was ordinarily conducted by seasoned ministers of standing. But many came to check out the meetings anyway, just to see how these young people would do. To their astonishment, this couple proved remarkably good preachers. They explained the gospel with a freshness and power the townspeople had never heard before. As a result, attendance grew, and everyone was talking about the wonderful truths of salvation and prophecy they were learning from these new preachers.

These events infuriated the lay leader of the town's largest church. He started up his own revival series, whose sole object was to counteract the influence and teachings of James and Ellen White. Learning from his friends what the young couple had preached the night before, this lay preacher would give a rousing discourse to refute everything they said. He insisted that they

were of the devil and were misleading souls. Among his accusations was that James and Ellen were preaching that we are saved
by obedience to the commandments. This was not true. They
taught that when we are saved by faith in Jesus, He brings us into
a new covenant relationship with Himself that enables us to keep
His law joyfully from the depths of a converted heart (see
Hebrews 8:10-12).

But their opposer would have none of it. He continued to twist
and vigorously misrepresent their position, making his central
assertion the unbiblical idea that Christ's death on the cross
resulted in the abolition of God's moral law. But then, in the
course of their teachings (and not as a rebuttal to their adversary) James and Ellen would bring out such texts as Matthew
5:19, 20; Romans 3:31; 7:12, 14; 8:4; 1 John 2:2-7; 3:24; 5:3;
Revelation 12:17; 14:12; and 22:14. But the preacher had ability
to speak with pathos and power. He would discourse on the
mercy, grace, and goodness of Christ and the all-covering merits of
Jesus' sacrifice. But his whole approach was to bring God's law and
grace into eternal enmity, as though they were at cross-purposes
with each other.

Among the people coming to James and Ellen's evangelistic
series was a young couple who were deeply attracted to their
messages. But they were perplexed. As members of the big
church in town, they felt obligated to go and listen to their elder
thundering away on alternate nights against the "new" teachings
and making impassioned appeals to the people to look away from
doctrine and only to the blood of Jesus. Deeply perplexed, this
couple came to James and Ellen White for a private conversation.

"When we hear you," the husband said, "everything you say
makes good biblical sense and our hearts are refreshed, but when
we hear our local preacher he also seems to make sense and uses
many Bible texts too. Since you and he take opposite positions on
so many vital points of Bible truth, you can't both be right. What
shall we do?"

James and Ellen did not want to pit themselves against their self-appointed antagonist. They were not there to attack churches or damage the reputation of others. They were simply seeking to do the work God had given them in helping to fulfill the great gospel commission of Matthew 28:18-20. Recognizing the high esteem in which this couple held their local religious leader, but also seeing how deeply they were drawn to the truth, Ellen and James prayed.

Although qualified to give a blow-by-blow refutation of the lay preacher, Ellen was distinctly impressed by an angel not to respond that way. Instead she said, "God will honor your search for truth. Keep reading your Bibles and come to the meetings. Within a month you will know beyond all doubt who is preaching the truth, and the way will be clear for you to understand all that God wants you to know."

Encouraged by this counsel, the young couple kept coming to James and Ellen's meetings, and also visited those of the local preacher. Meanwhile, James and Ellen prayed that God would vindicate His own truth.

Several weeks later, while the no-law preacher was thundering against James and Ellen for their alleged heresies, he was seized with a horrible pain in his stomach and had to be assisted from the platform and taken to a doctor. Having ruptured a blood vessel in his stomach, he was confined to bed, where he was making a slow and uncertain recovery. During this time he could not carry out his duties as town manager and treasurer. Prior to this he had exclusive oversight of the accounts, and the books had never been audited. The town council appointed an assistant, who felt that it was his first duty to go through the books and see that the accounts were in order. To his astonishment, he discovered a thousand-dollar discrepancy between the books and the bank account. He reported his findings to the council, which deemed it best to send him, along with a couple of deputies from the sheriff's department, to discover the reason for this mysterious shortfall in the town's bank balance. Although suspicious, they did not come to accuse the preacher, but simply to inquire. He was, after all, a man of great stature in the community and a respected churchman.

As they approached the preacher's house one of the deputies saw his wife run out the back door to the barn with a bulging sack in her hand. He decided to watch her movements while the interim treasurer and the other deputy came into the sick man's room. In response to their apologetic inquiry about the missing money, he sat up in bed and raising his right hand solemnly, intoned, "I swear on my honor before the God of heaven, that I did not steal that money, nor do I know anything about it." His wife, who had just returned from her quick trip to the barn, thinking she had gone unobserved, also insisted that her husband was innocent of any wrongdoing.

Just then the other deputy burst into the room holding a large sack he had retrieved from the barn, and exclaimed, "What's this?" The sack contained the missing money, which the elder's wife had rushed to hide in their barn. The elder's disgrace was quickly blazed all over town. Needless to say, that annihilated his influence and exposed the fatal error of his no-law theology. The anxious young couple then recognized the veracity of all that James and Ellen had been so faithfully preaching and teaching, and unhesitatingly took their stand for the truth.

❦ ❦ ❦ ❦

It happened in Uganda during the brutal, blood-soaked days of Idi Amin's dictatorship. So ruthless and violent was his regime that torture and death were the decreed fate of all who took exception to his policies of suppression of everything decent and progressive. Lawyers and other professionals walked to work wearing ragged clothing and battered tennis shoes in order not to be seized and summarily executed as enemies of the state, just because they looked well educated and wore European-style clothing.

Despite suffering persecution from Amin's military thugs, true Christians remained faithful to God. He did not desert His people. Isaiah's words from the Lord proved true on their behalf, as they have for believers in every generation and will to the close of time: "For He said, 'Surely they are My people, children who will not lie.' So He became their Savior. In all their affliction He was afflicted, and the Angel of His Presence saved them; in His love and in His pity He redeemed them; and He bore them and carried them all the days of old" (Isaiah 63:8, 9). Angels hovered over Uganda during the bleakest two-year period of its entire history. They were there to dispel the darkness and bring deliverance at the crucial hour.

Robert Kiwanuka, a Christian journalist in Kampala, Uganda, filed this story a little over twenty years ago.

For 569 days between 1977 and 1979, Seventh-day Adventists in Uganda were placed in "spiritual captivity" after their church and several others were banned. Soon after the ban, pastors in their areas formed church groups in various Adventist homes.

During that difficult time the Lord led His people. Some believers experienced difficulties, including imprisonment and beatings, but this did not discourage the Adventists. Instead, it strengthened their faith. Also strengthening their faith were the miracles they saw performed in their behalf.

One miracle happened when 20 mysterious men sought an audience with President Idi Amin at the State House in Entebbe. It was reported from the State House that the men approached the main gate and told the heavily armed guards that they wanted to meet the president. It could easily have meant one's life just to approach the gate without authorization.

"Did you make arrangements to have an audience with the president?" one of the guards sternly demanded.

"We've made no arrangements with the president, but we'll have to meet with him," the men confidently replied. No appointment and no printed credentials meant absolutely no admittance into the presidential palace. Yet the guards found themselves inexplicably yielding to the influence of these men, and allowed them into the State House unannounced.

The men entered the visitors' room, and the president was

called in. Wasting no time, they told him they were Seventh-day Adventists and had come to request freedom to worship in their churches. Shocked by this unprecedented intrusion, he asked whether they had made their request to the Department of Religious Affairs. Seizing his phone he quickly dialed the head of that department, who replied that she had never seen or heard of such persons in her office.

Turning to the men, the president abruptly said he had no time to talk with them. "But we will remain Seventh-day Adventists," one of the men firmly stated as he looked unwaveringly at the president. They left his office and were not seen again by any of the guards or State House personnel. How they left remained a mystery. Undoubtedly, Amin tried to have the men arrested, but they were beyond his reach or authority.

When the report of this visit reached Adventist headquarters in Kireka, the leaders there diligently inquired as to who could have made this visit. Not a clue turned up among any of the pastors or churches. They could attribute this mysterious event only to the visitation of angels coming to restrain Amin's demonic hostility to the church, and appeal to him as to Pharaoh before his self-inflicted downfall from oppressing God's people. Certainly this report gave a great boost to the morale of Ugandan Adventists. They knew that the Lord was among them and had seen their affliction. They felt sure that he would soon undertake their deliverance, and they were right.

Another of the many miracles during these dark and difficult days happened when a district pastor was arrested, along with about thirty-five believers who had been worshiping in a private house. They were taken to a prison, where an officer ordered a guard to lock up twenty-five of them.

The prison guard put them in a room and tried to shut the door. He could not move it, although it was free on its hinges. He applied more force, but it would not close. He called a fellow guard to help him, but they could not force the door shut even by the utmost exertion. Compelled to leave the door open, the guards stood on the other side of it, glowering at their "prisoners."

To break the tension, the Adventists began singing and then decided to pray. Wanting to pray undisturbed, the pastor pulled the "immovable" door gently and closed it without effort. In shame and frustration, the Ugandan authorities were forced to release the prisoners whom they could not lock up or compel to abandon their faith. Not long after these incidents Idi Amin's government collapsed, and he was forced to flee Uganda, never to return.[1]

❦ ❦ ❦ ❦

God does not exercise His justice with intent to destroy us but to awaken the erring to their spiritual offensiveness and to protect the faithful. An interesting example of this takes us back to the days when Mountain View College, the School of the Light, in Bukidnon, Philippines was being established in 1949. Pastor Adriel Chilson tells the story.

During the period of World War II when the Japanese Imperial Army had complete control of the Philippine towns and cities, many Adventists were forced to hide in the mountains. Their pastors went with them. From time to time officers of the Mindanao Mission carried on risky visitation in these regions. One extensive itinerary took A. G. Macasiano, D. B. Ladion, and A. N. Somoso past a beautiful plateau with a hill standing nearby.

"What an ideal place for a school!" Pastor Macasiano exclaimed.

"But who would ever come here, anyway?" Pastor Somoso questioned.

"Well, our Filipino students go as far as Europe and America. Why not have them come here?"

"That's right," agreed Pastor Ladion. "Let's pray that God will preserve this property for us."

But when liberation came, the leaders were so busy building up the churches that the site and the prayer for it were forgotten. The years brought many changes. In 1947 Pastor Macasiano was transferred to the South-Central Luzon Mission, and there he met Dr. Andrew N. Nelson, first postwar president of Philippine Union College. While visiting together one day, Nelson asked where a large tract of land could be found for a college farm.

"How many hectares do you need?" Macasiano asked.

"Six hundred or perhaps a thousand."

"I know of such a place on Mindanao."

"How do I get there?" Dr. Nelson inquired.

"Easily. At our Mindanao Mission headquarters, ask for a man to guide you to Bag-ong Taas, Malaybalay, Bukidnon. The church elder there will take you to a tableland in the hills just north of the village." Two years passed before Dr. Nelson was able to go to Mindanao. Accompanied by the union and Far Eastern Division educational secretaries, he looked over the general area, but discovered much cogon grass there. Though excellent for roofing homes, this grass is difficult to eradicate. The men returned to Bag-ong Taas almost disheartened.

The next morning at breakfast, the local church elder told them that during the night he had dreamed of a beautiful table-land up north of the village, and farther on, a lake and a high waterfall in an area of thick forest. Startled, division educational secretary W. O. Baldwin exclaimed, "Say, I had exactly the same dream!"

The group hurriedly prepared lunches and began the upland trip. Seeing a lone hill rising above the rolling countryside, they decided to climb it. From the top they viewed the plateau of their dreams, the same one that had been picked and prayed for seven years earlier. But problems still lay ahead.

After the property had been secured and a few students settled there to begin construction, a rich and influential man in Bukidnon Province filed a trespassing accusation, claiming the land as part of his pasture concession. He petitioned the Bureau of Agriculture for ejection of the Adventists. But the secretary for the Bureau ruled in favor of the school, saying that the education of youth took priority over pasturing cattle.

Failing in his attempts, the accuser began to use harassment and coercion, especially after the school opened. But God was watching over His work. One night two jeep-loads of armed men, intending to drive the students and teachers from the new campus, started for the school. But as they drove up the steep road leading to the college, a giant barred their path and threatened to roll their jeeps over the precipice along the edge of the road if they did not turn back.

One of the raiders returned to the college the next day to find out about the giant who guarded the institution at night. When he was told that there was none, he left deeply impressed that a superhuman power had protected the school.[2]

Truly, the Lord does give His angels charge over us not only as protectors and providers, but as ministers of justice and upholders of His divine law and will. No wonder the psalmist fervently proclaimed, "Bless the Lord, ye his angels, that excel in strength, . . . hearkening unto the voice of his word. Bless ye the Lord, all ye his hosts; ye ministers of his, that do his pleasure" (Psalm 103:20, 21, KJV).

---

1. Adapted from *Adventist Review*, September 20, 1979, p. 23.
2. Adapted from *When God Provides*, by Adriel D. Chilson, Review and Herald, 1994. pp. 137, 138.

# CHAPTER ELEVEN

# *Angels in War Time*

ngels are no strangers to war. As incongruous as it sounds, the first war ever fought was in heaven. John writes in the book of Revelation, "War broke out in heaven: Michael and his angels fought against the dragon; and the dragon and his angels fought, but they did not prevail, nor was a place found for them in heaven any longer" (Revelation 12:7, 8).

How did heaven become the first battlefield? It all began with Lucifer, the highest-ranking angel who defected because of pride over his vast abilities and power. Ezekiel 28 and Isaiah 14 tell the story. Egotism, power hunger, jealousy over his subordination to the Godhead and especially to Jesus, the co-creator of the Universe with His Father and the Holy Spirit—all these factors combined to promote rebellion in Lucifer's heart.

It did not have to be that way. Physically and mentally, Lucifer was created perfect. God gave Him a flawless education. Heaven's laws were reasonable then as they are now. Living conditions were perfect—no poverty, sickness, disease, inequity, no harsh rule, unreasonable requirements, or arbitrary exercise of power on God's part. But one thing God would not do was to create His intelligent beings to give Him preprogrammed loyalty and praise.

Instead He endowed angels and other cosmic intelligent beings with innate powers to grow mentally and morally and to exercise freedom of choice. True, all were created to harmonize naturally with God's character and will, but this inborn bent to obey was to be sustained voluntarily by each being, rather than maintained by coercion. Plainly put, any being at any time could choose to disobey God and strike out on a path of independence. Never would God give any provocation to that, not even by being uncommunicative about the goodness of His ways and laws. God has always been generously self-revealing, always willing to communicate with His creatures.

When Lucifer rebelled, God did not leave him or the angels in the dark about the terrible results that would follow from his departure from the right way. Lucifer had launched an elaborate campaign to misrepresent God to the angels. One can readily deduce from his brash rantings recorded in Isaiah 14 that his complaints included allegations of tyranny on God's part, unfairness in His law, and suppression of personal liberty. The fact that he was able to ensnare a third of the angels, who all knew what God is really like, should warn us that Satan's powers of deception are very great. It should also convince us that we need to fully trust God and submit to His grace and authority if we want to be rescued from the horrible effects of sin and rebellion.

Scripture tells us that God does not change. Therefore we can safely assume that prior to open warfare in heaven, God did everything within the reach of His infinite love and wisdom to call Lucifer back from his subversive alienation. The loyal angels undoubtedly did all they could to dissuade Lucifer and his angel followers from their growing moral madness. Each angel was free to choose masters, Lucifer or Christ. Lucifer's defiance mounted;

his charges grew more strident and desperate. He forced a show-down. Then war erupted in heaven. The arch-rebel and his followers were cast out.

We might ask, why didn't God simply destroy Satan, once his hostility to truth and love became so apparent? We must remember that sin was a new factor in the universe. Not even the loyal angels could fully conceive of its final effects. And since God's trustworthiness had been called into question by Satan, the Lord deemed it wisest to allow this adversary to act out his plans in full so that everyone could trace the course of sin from its seemingly innocuous beginnings to its truly devastating end. That is why Paul identified this planet as the theater of the universe, viewed by angels and men (see 1 Corinthians 4:9). By seeing Satan fully exhibit his character and purposes, all could see beyond question that no justification can be found for disobedience to God, and no good results can come of it. Thus the universe is rendered sin-proof.

Having successfully participated in expelling Satan and his rebellious hosts from heaven, God's angels are adept at ministering to people in war-torn lands.

At Darventa, Serbia in 1992, Philip and a band of six teenagers were pinned down under the crossfire of opposing armies. Philip and his friends belonged to no faction. They only wished for peace in their land. But now they were in desperate need of shelter—anywhere free from the relentless shelling and bombing that threatened to destroy the whole town.

Crawling along the besieged hillside, Philip and his friends headed to a bombed-out building that offered at least the protection of a ragged portion of roof, brick walls, and a few battered rooms whose masonry hadn't yet collapsed. Night had fallen, and the young men began exploring the layout of their new shelter. Soon they discovered a large room with chairs lined up in rows facing a slightly elevated platform. Being Muslims and unfamiliar with Christian meeting places, it took them a while to discover that they were in a Protestant church. This place, a

Seventh-day Adventist church, was their shelter for the next two months.

One of the least damaged rooms had books and pictures for children. Eventually the boys concluded that this was a place of worship, and they chose to treat it with reverence. Sensing that the pulpit and organ were connected with sacred service, the boys always kept back from that area. A small closet-like space near the front door was nearly intact. Accordingly, the boys selected it as a post for sentry duty, which they shared on a rotating schedule. Around the walls of this little room were shelves stacked with books, some of which were bullet ridden.

Finding a Bible in the collection, Philip began to read but got bogged down after the first three chapters of Genesis. Spotting a book entitled *The Great Controversy,* Philip became curious and pulled it from the shelf. The very name of the book seemed pertinent to the circumstances they were in. Galvanized by the prophetic message of this book that described world conditions with which he was all too familiar, Philip read through the book. When he returned the book to the shelf, Philip noticed the address of the publishing house in Belgrade. Because of the unusual street name given, this address stayed in his memory.

From time to time the boys had to venture forth from their battered shelter to find food and water. Unable to use the door because it was vulnerable to sniper fire, Philip had to crawl through a side window frame, above which hung a picture of Christ with outstretched hands and the inscription "Come Unto Me." This picture and its invitation irritated Philip. "How can I believe in a God of mercy and love in this violence-racked world, where I could be cut down by bullets any moment, day after day?"

Then came his turn to search for supplies. Just as he was about to climb out the window, Philip heard an unfamiliar voice call his name aloud directly behind him. Stepping back quickly from the window, he turned around to look for the caller but saw no one. At that moment a volley of gunfire shattered the window frame and pocked the walls. Without recognizing its identity, Philip had just been rescued by his guardian angel from being shot. But it was clear to him and his companions that they had been discovered. Flight was now imperative.

Sensing that a divine call had been in the voice that warned him from going through the window, Philip prayed for a lull in the shelling so that he and his companions could make their way to safety. No sooner had he prayed than the shelling stopped. Seizing the moment, Philip shouted to his companions, "This is the sign. It's time for us to escape now." Clambering out the window, they all raced down the hillside into the shattered city, while the gunfire following them from behind fell short of its mark.

Several months later the war ended. Tired, dispirited and emaciated, Philip decided to try contacting his sister Suada, who had escaped from their town about a year earlier to live with their grandparents in another city. But she was not there. A thin trail of leads finally placed in his possession the telephone number of a school near the city of Marusavec, where someone thought she might be staying as a refugee.

To his joy, Philip reached Suada by phone, and learned from her that she was very happy in her new location. "This place is too nice for me to describe to you over the phone. You must come and see it for yourself," she said.

Philip received a very cordial welcome from the people at the school, where Suada was enrolled as a student. Never had he seen her so happy before. Suada shared with Philip some of the books she was reading at the school. To his astonishment he saw on the flyleaf of a book the same address in Belgrade that he had seen in so many of the bullet-ridden books on the shelves of his hiding place in Darventa. Now he felt impelled to study the literature and religion that had come to mean so much to his beloved sister. He enrolled for the next semester at this school, called the Murasavec Adventist Seminary. As a college graduate in electrical engineering, he had little difficulty in catching up with all the studies. Biblical Greek and theology were new to this young Muslim man, but he proved an apt student, and found himself drawn to the Adventist faith.

Later, during a visit to the Central Adventist Church in Zagreb he met a young woman by the name of Blanka. After they got to know each other, love blossomed between them. In 1994 Philip was baptized into the Adventist church, and he also married Blanka. He and Blanka have gone back to Darventa, where they are now working to rebuild and restore the bombed-out church that was once his shelter. It is now Philip's ambition to help people find refuge, not from bombs and bullets, but from sin, by taking refuge in the Savior, Jesus, whose angel rescued Philip and has protected him through his beleaguered odyssey to redemption.[1]

❦ ❦ ❦ ❦

Angels are not afraid of man's death-dealing plans and devices. Only in eternity will we know fully how vitally they have been involved in fending off Satan's war against humanity fought with weapons both visible and invisible.

On a hill overlooking the Adventist mission station, hundreds of angry local inhabitants gathered at twilight by Piata Bay on Lake Titicaca, Peru. Blowing horns and beating drums, they began to yell and shriek like demons. Knowing that this was the signal for a murderous night, villagers desperately ran to the mission for protection. But what could the missionaries do?

Many years before, Pastor Gilbert had taken charge of the Adventist mission on this beautiful inland bay. Here the villagers learned about Jesus and built a little adobe house of worship. All went well until the populace in the surrounding mountains became angry because White people had been taking their lands. It was time to drive them out or kill them before the takeover was complete.

So several hundred Indians with drums, horns, clubs, and knives gathered on the ridge top above the village. As their chorus of war chants swelled, Pastor Gilbert invited all the villagers who wanted protection to come into the church building.

Suddenly all the yelling on the hilltop ceased, and the drums fell silent. Not a single warrior came down the hill. The people were thankful to be spared in answer to their prayers.

The next night it happened again, and once again the Indians did not come down. On the third night the warriors returned with reinforcements. But they retreated as before.

On the fourth night an even larger number of warriors assembled, yelling, tooting, and pounding with fresh intensity. They spread across the entire length of the ridge like a huge scythe. Their ferocious yells suggested that they intended to carry out their business. Soon they marched downhill to the accompaniment of war whoops and the clangor of weapons. They swooped down with increasing speed, but suddenly stopped in their tracks and stared at the lake. In an instant they turned around and frantically fled over the ridge, never to return.

The next day the villagers were surprised to find horns, drums, knives, and ponchos scattered across the hillside. The combatants had left them in their mad flight. But why had they run away? Several weeks went by with the mystery still unexplained.

Then one day a few unfamiliar Indians came down to the mission station. Peering cautiously about, they asked Pastor Gilbert, "Where do you keep your soldiers?"

"We have no soldiers," replied Pastor Gilbert.

"Oh, but you have many, many soldiers. We know. They must be hiding in the bushes."

Pastor Gilbert gave them permission to look all around the mission, including the house and church. After a diligent search the head of this little party came back to Pastor Gilbert and said, "We don't understand. About a month ago we came to attack the mission and kill everyone in it. But then we saw soldiers hiding in the bushes around the mission. We decided to wait until the next night and bring more fighters. But that night we saw twice as many soldiers protecting your place. On the third night we brought back hundreds more men, but as we overlooked the village, it seemed to be swarming with soldiers.

"Finally, we decided to assemble 2,000 warriors, thinking that we could overwhelm all your soldiers and kill you. But as we came down the hill to attack, not only did we see all the soldiers you had before, but also a brilliantly lighted ship that flew across Lake Titicaca like a swift-moving bird. Soon it stopped at the beach, and out poured thousands of soldiers carrying guns and boxes of ammunition. With terrific speed they all marched in rank past the mission and surged up the hill, where we all stood fearful and trembling. Finally we turned and ran for our lives, leaving everything behind so that we could escape more quickly."

Pastor Gilbert explained that these were angels of heaven who had come to the rescue of the villagers and the mission. As a result of this report, many of the would-be murderers came to the mission to learn how to worship the great God who had so strikingly delivered His people.

❦ ❦ ❦ ❦

Angels are primarily in the business of trying to bring people to the Savior, including those with the most hateful and misguided intentions. Our last story in this chapter illustrates God's use of human beings and angels working in partnership to turn the tide of events in wartime in an unexpected manner that brings glory to God.

Bandit, killer, rebel chief—Peter was a terror to the countryside in the central African nation where he resided. His cruel raids and destructive actions prompted the government to offer a huge reward for his capture, dead or alive. Government troops were annihilated when they attempted to advance through Peter's territory deep in the jungle. Then the UN sent in two detachments of soldiers renowned for stamina and bravery. Only a few men returned alive from each of these separate operations to tell the tale of Peter's devastating ambushes.

The villages under Peter's jurisdiction lived in constant terror of his raids for scarce supplies. The situation had grown so bad that a whole section of the country was deprived of medicines, vital foodstuffs, and other critical supplies. But who could enter the danger zone?

One day Pastor Robinson received a call from the nation's president. The two men were good friends. The president outlined to Pastor Robinson the situation with which the whole country was familiar, adding details that had not been publicized. The situation was dangerous and grim. Would Pastor Robinson be willing to guide a convoy of government trucks on a peace mission bearing medicines and other critically needed supplies to the area under Peter's control? As a missionary familiar with that territory, Robinson might have a better chance of delivering these items than a government official would.

Realizing the risk involved, Pastor Robinson asked for time to pray with his colleagues. Soon the answer came to him in the form of a distinctly remembered Bible promise: "For He shall give His angels charge over you, to keep you in all your ways. They shall bear you up in their hands, lest you dash your foot against a stone" (Psalm 91:11, 12).

A hundred tons of supplies were flown into an airport closest to the stricken area, then loaded onto 17 trucks and 3 jeeps. Looking at Pastor Robinson sadly and seriously, as though it might be for the last time, the president said, "Be careful. But God is with you."

Pastor Robinson worked closely with the military for determining the best time to traverse a long valley and ascend a steep mountain, beyond which was the territory designated to receive the supplies. The whole length of the journey carried the risk of detection by the Terror's reconnaissance men. After five days' wait it seemed safe to go.

As the convoy slowly wound its way through the valley, they were aghast to see the whole way strewn with corpses of those who had fallen victim to the Terror's insatiable blood-lust.

Pastor Robinson went in the lead jeep. Peter, his assigned driver, was a dedicated Christian and a member of the Terror's tribe, though loyal to the established government. He knew the language and customs, as did Pastor Robinson, because he had worked in that territory some years before. Finally, they passed through the valley and completed the laborious ascent up the mountain, which they had been told was safe at the top and on the wide plateau beyond. They breathed a prayer of relief.

Knowing that it would take the trucks behind them another half hour or so to lumber up the hill, Robinson and Peter decided to go on to the village that lay ahead. They proceeded on the one road that stretched before them through the plain and jungle on both sides. It was as they passed through one of these jungle groves that Peter jerked the wheel to one side and ran the vehicle into a ditch.

"Why did you do that?" Robinson asked in consternation.

"Oh, pastor, I have seen the sign. It's the Terror's secret sign—a white feather tied to a branch overhead. This is the sign of my tribe to give a last warning of danger and death ahead. We will be killed, Pastor Robinson. The Terror is here. I just know it."

Pastor Robinson climbed out of the vehicle. An eerie silence engulfed the jungle. Fresh tracks lay in the road, but there was no detectable movement. Pastor Robinson had the distinct sense that he was being watched. Putting a radio microphone to his mouth, he said, in the language of the tribe, "We have come as friends. I am a servant of God. I am here to help you. Anybody in this area who needs help, please do not be afraid. We are not here as enemies but as friends."

Nothing happened. It remained deathly calm and still. Then suddenly Pastor Robinson heard the *snap! snap!* of two dry twigs rapidly broken. It was a signal that he had learned as a boy. It was a challenge that demanded a reply. A special password must be spoken, known only to members or close friends of the tribe. But what was the password? It had been more than fifteen years since Pastor Robinson had heard it. He prayed. As words came winging back into his mind, he spoke them quickly and sharply, according to the tribal custom.

Then Pastor Robinson saw a tall, majestic figure slowly emerge from the jungle, pointing a rifle straight at his chest. The man kept advancing. Pastor Robinson gave a respectful greeting. Slowly the man lowered his gun and continued his approach. Robinson extended his hand. In response the man clasped his hand and said in surprise, "Pastor Robinson! What are you doing here?"

Utterly astonished, Robinson scrutinized the man's face. Decorated as it was with war paint and markings, he could not tell the man's identity. "Do you know me?" he asked.

"Yes, of course I know you. Don't you know me?"

"Who are you?"

"I am the Terror. But you know me by another name. I am Henry from the village of Wait. You used to teach us in your little branch Sabbath School thirteen or fifteen years ago. I am your pupil, Henry. Don't you remember me?"

Of course he did. And the boy Henry was this feared bandit, with a large price on his head!

And now Henry stood before him, holding onto Pastor Robinson's hand and shaking like a leaf in the wind. His whole body shook uncontrollably. In awed tones, Henry said, "Now I understand. Now I understand. For the first time in my life I lost my voice. It was taken from me. As you went into the ditch I tried to order my men to kill you, but I could not speak. My voice failed me. And as I looked at the wheels spinning around on your jeep, I could see soldiers standing around, heavily armed. I could see these soldiers also coming up the road directly behind you. They didn't look like any soldiers I have ever seen."

He went on, almost rhapsodically, "Now I understand. Those stories you used to tell us, those picture rolls you used to show us—of your God, and of those angels that God sends to help His people." He was still trembling. "Now I understand. Those beings that looked like the moon and the stars as they guarded you were angels from your God. Oh, Pastor Robinson! What are you doing here?"

What an inspiration and encouragement to the pastor! His

own fears vanished as he heard Henry's remarkable account. For while Pastor Robinson had not seen these angels, he knew that they were still standing right there beside them, controlling the situation. Over the next two or three minutes the pastor explained his mission to the still trembling Henry.

As they talked, the rumble of the delivery trucks became distinctly audible. "Pastor, are there soldiers in those trucks?" Henry asked with fright.

"Yes, Henry, but they are under my control. They are under my orders."

"Oh, but will they kill me?"

He knew of the huge reward to bring him in dead or alive. But the pastor assured him, "There will be no killing here today. God and His angels are here. We are working together to save lives, not to kill."

Though getting louder, the trucks were still some distance away, and the pastor took this opportunity to plead with Henry for his salvation. "Friend, you have seen today a wonderful demonstration of God's love for you. I did not see those angel soldiers, but you did, and you know that just one of those angels could have annihilated you and your men. They didn't, because God loves you. That same Jesus you heard about under the trees in Wait fifteen years ago is still speaking to you. Promise me, Henry, that you will give up this life of destruction, looting, and killing; promise me that you will respect and honor the love of Jesus who has saved your life, and who wants to give you eternal life with Him."

Still trembling, he hesitated and looked around. The pastor then asked him to call his men forth from the jungle. Henry gave an order, and dozens of heavily armed bandits came out from both sides of the jungle. They couldn't understand what had happened to their proud and haughty leader who grasped the hand of a white man, a member of the race they were sworn to destroy. They stared at Robinson with cruelty and hatred in their eyes.

As his men closed in on the scene, Henry said to them, "This man's skin is white, but his heart is with us. He is our friend."

As they gathered around him, Henry told his compatriots about losing his voice, seeing the angel soldiers, and his pastor friend's assurance that these angel guards were still there watching everything.

Then Robinson asked him again, "Henry, will you promise to give up this terrible life of destruction and slaughter?" And there, in the presence of his men, he promised.

Moments before the convoy rounded the bend, Henry and his soldiers receded back into the jungle, to be seen no more. Robinson and the government soldiers carried out their mission of peace without further interference.

Understandably, it took many months for the government to be convinced that the danger was permanently ended, and that the Terror was a converted man. But the killing and plunder stopped completely. Then an official proclamation was issued, explaining briefly that the Terror was now a Christian and so the price on his head was no longer an offer. The radio blared the news. The newspapers carried it in the headlines. For many people, hope in God dawned from the ending of this dark episode.

The lessons we learn from angels in time of war carry down to all of us. He who put to flight armies and put to rest the wrath of armed and angry men is able to protect us in our times of crisis. He can use us to bear witness to His mighty power not only to deliver us from danger but to save the most determined of His enemies, if only they will yield to His unveiled love.

---

1. Adapted from an article by Don Jacobsen in *Adventist Review*, Jan. 1999.

# CHAPTER TWELVE

# *Dreams and Visions*

**A**ngels serve as God's messengers. Sometimes they have the best access to us in our dreams, when we are freed from the distractions of daily life and are lifted above our barriers of pragmatism and doubt. We must always remember, however, that no angel of God will ever lead us contrary to Scripture or give special revelations that supersede His written Word. Angels assist God in teaching us divine law and its all-encompassing applications to life. They do not teach us to bypass or minimize Scripture, but lead us to revere that unalterable source of holy instruction (see Deuteronomy 33:2; Acts 7:53).

In 1846 Annie and her brother, Uriah, were away at school. They had been part of the great Advent movement until late 1844, but Annie and Uriah had begun to lose interest in spiritual things. Being bright and ambitious, they wanted worldly success.

But their mother, Rebecca, still believed in Jesus' soon coming. She had become a Sabbath keeper through

*161*

hearing Captain Joseph Bates preach. Mrs. Smith prayed that her children would come back to Jesus.

One day Captain Bates told Mrs. Smith, "I'm going to preach in Somerville, Massachusetts in a few days."

"Oh," exclaimed Mrs. Smith, "that's near Annie's school. I'll write and ask her to go to your meeting."

As Annie read her mother's letter she thought, *The meeting will be this Saturday. I'm free then, so just to please my mother I will go.*

The night before the meeting, Annie had a dream. She saw herself coming to the meeting late, while a hymn was being sung. She sat in the only empty seat at the back of the room. When the hymn ended, a tall, noble-looking man walked over to a chart full of pictures and said, "Unto two thousand and three hundred days, then shall the sanctuary be cleansed." In her dream Annie understood and believed his explanation of the prophecy from Daniel.

The same night in which Annie dreamed this, Captain Bates dreamed that he was to preach on Daniel's great time prophecy. As the last hymn was being sung, he saw a young woman enter the room and sit in the only seat left. As he preached about the twenty-three-hundred-day prophecy of Daniel 8:14, he saw her listening intently and agreeing with his message.

The next evening Annie started out early for the meeting, but took a wrong turn and lost her way. When she found the right house, the people inside were singing a hymn. She quietly took the last seat at the back of the room shortly before the preacher arose to speak. When the hymn ended, Captain Bates stood up and walked over to his picture chart and began, "Unto two thousand and three hundred days . . ."

When the meeting ended, Captain Bates went straight to Annie and said, "You are Annie, the daughter of Rebecca Smith, aren't you? I dreamed about you last night." Annie said, "I dreamed about you, and heard in my dream the same message that you preached tonight! I know that your message is true because it's just what the Bible teaches."

That night Annie decided to follow the whole truth, including the Sabbath. Shortly afterward, Uriah made the same commitment.

Both Annie and Uriah gave up offers of high-paying jobs and popularity, to serve instead with the poor, struggling Adventist group, without wages or worldly honor. Annie wrote beautiful hymns, some of which Christians still sing today. She was also the first female editor of the *Adventist Review* (then called *The Advent Review and Sabbath Herald*). Annie died when she was only 26. Uriah edited the *Adventist Review* for 50 years and also wrote many excellent books, including one on Daniel and Revelation, which is still widely read by Bible students.

Note that Annie was not guided exclusively by her dream. She embraced the truth because it was so clearly explained from the Bible. Her dream was a sign, but not the foundation of her faith. Ultimately, dreams from God can only benefit those who are willing to walk in His truth during their waking hours.

❦ ❦ ❦ ❦

Some years ago Chit Hla, an Adventist evangelist in Rangoon (now called Yangon), Myamar, met a young dentist who had attended a mission school sponsored by a major denomination. When he graduated from that school he wondered whether to join the church that was sponsoring the mission, or to continue as a Buddhist. His search for truth was earnest, and he found both religions to be unsatisfactory. Yet he became increasingly convinced that Christianity was true.

Then one night in a dream he saw two men dressed in white coming to his house. He heard a voice declare, "These men will lead you to the way of truth and peace." In his dream he asked which was the true church. The answer was, "The true church will tell you about prophecy."

Chit Hla tells the rest of the story:

"For two or three months the dentist thought over this strange dream. Then one day, one of my helpers, Maung Potok, and I, traveling along the road, canvassing, came near to the dentist's home. We were dressed completely in white. The dentist came along the road and saw us. Greeting him, I asked, 'Where are you going?'

" 'I am on my business as a dentist. Who are you?'

" 'I am the new doctrine preacher,' I replied.

" 'Can you tell me about prophecy?' asked the dentist.

" 'Yes,' we said.

"Remembering his dream about the two men in white who would explain prophecy and lead him to the truth, the dentist became very interested. He arranged for us to come to his house as soon as his business was done. We came at the appointed time.

" 'Now,' he said, 'I am waiting to hear. Can you tell me about the new world Ruler who is coming?'"

Chit Hla opened his Bible to Daniel 2 and gave an explanation of the prophecy. When the evangelist finished, the dentist declared, "You are the man I saw in a dream!" Shortly afterward he was baptized and became a preacher of the truth.[1]

❦ ❦ ❦ ❦

Scripture helps us to understand the purpose of dreams. In Job, the oldest book in the Bible, we read a description of how God sometimes works to preserve people from making fatal mistakes.

> For God may speak in one way, or in another, yet man does not perceive it. In a dream, in a vision of the night, when deep sleep falls upon men, while slumbering on their beds, when He opens the ears of men, and seals their instruction. In order to turn man from his deed, and conceal pride from man, He keeps back his soul from the pit, and his life from perishing by the sword . . . that he may be enlightened with the light of life (Job 33:14-18, 30, NKJV).

And that Light, of course, is Christ, who declared, " 'I am the Light of the world. He who follows Me shall not walk in darkness, but shall have the light of life' " (John 8:12). It is always

Jesus' plan to lead us into light that will prepare us for citizenship in His kingdom (see Proverbs 4:18; 1 John 1:7; Revelation 18:1-4).

Glenn Aufderhar of the Adventist Media Center recently told the story of a mother and daughter in Romania who were attending a full gospel message evangelistic series. Each lived in different locations in the city. The mother, whom we shall call Eustacia, lived several miles from the meeting hall, but the daughter, Ana, lived only a few blocks away. Both mother and daughter were deeply stirred by the meetings, but began to feel many fears and doubts as the beautiful truths they were learning night by night came into collision with certain religious traditions and beliefs that they had held dear all their lives. They saw that the evangelist was presenting pure Bible truth, but it differed so markedly from what their priests taught. Both mother and daughter seriously thought about dropping out of the meetings after the next night's presentation, especially if it contained anything additional that conflicted with their familiar beliefs.

During the night the mother slept uneasily. Then she was awakened by the appearance of a light in her room. Looking toward the light she saw a majestic person in a white suit holding an open Bible in his hand. She was not afraid of the person standing there, because she clearly sensed that he would do no harm. From her position in the bed she looked intently at the page of the Bible to which the mysterious visitor was pointing. The passage was Exodus 20. Verses 8-11 were illuminated with a soft golden light that gave special prominence to the words, which stated the Sabbath commandment. She read the words, being especially impressed by the thought that the seventh day was the Sabbath. Then the silent visitor disappeared. Aroused by this vision, Eustacia looked forward to the next evening's meeting.

Leaving earlier than usual for the meeting hall that evening, Eustacia gathered neighbors and passing strangers about her to tell them of her amazing experience the night before. Many of these people joined her in a veritable march to the meeting hall.

En route, Eustacia announced to her impromptu entourage that she must stop at her daughter's apartment to have her join them in their trek to the meeting. Eustacia did not need to go up the stairs. As she approached her daughter's apartment building, Ana came bounding out, her face all aglow. She said, "Mother, you'll never guess what happened to me last night."

Eustacia said, "Tell us, we all want to hear."

Without hesitation Ana related an experience identical to her mother's. Recognizing that this had not been planned ahead by mother and daughter, curiosity mounted in the group. They all entered the meeting hall together.

The evangelist's subject that night? God's true day of worship. Eustacia and Ana's reservations and doubts vanished, and they continued to drink in Bible truth night by night. They were baptized to join God's commandment-keeping people at the end of the series, and have been active witnesses for the Lord ever since.

We could tell many similar stories of recent origin. Why? Because the Bible prophesies that shortly before Jesus returns, " 'it shall come to pass . . . that I will pour out My Spirit on all flesh; your sons and your daughters shall prophesy, your old men shall dream dreams, your young men shall see visions; and also on My menservants and on My maidservants I will pour out My Spirit in those days. And it shall come to pass that whoever calls on the name of the Lord shall be saved. For in Mount Zion and in Jerusalem there shall be deliverance, as the Lord has said, among the remnant whom the Lord calls' " (Joel 2:28, 29, 32).

❦ ❦ ❦ ❦

Crystal N. of Reno, Nevada sent us an account of a compelling dream sent from heaven to awaken her to present truth in preparation for Jesus' soon return. Crystal writes:

"I had wandered away from God and church. On December 1, 1993, after my husband had gone to work at 8:00 A.M., I went back to bed and soon fell asleep and dreamed that I was with a group of people standing in a field and gazing up into the sky. Far above we saw three white birds approaching us in a zigzag flight pattern across the sky. Someone in the crowd said in astonishment, "One of those birds is saying something!" As the three figures in flight came closer we all saw that they were not birds, but angels.

"Someone behind me said, 'The three angels' messages!' I turned my head to see who had spoken, but could not determine who it was. Looking back up into the sky I noticed that the angels were now directly overhead. They stopped in midair, remaining stationary for a while, and then swooped down to where we stood. Someone holding a microphone dashed up to them and excitedly blurted out, 'Are you aliens?' One of the angels quietly took up the would-be reporter and placed him back in the crowd. Then, addressing all of us assembled there, the angels solemnly stated, 'We have a message for you. Jesus is coming very, very soon.'

"Startled, I awoke from my dream. The outcome of this experience is that I have come back to the Lord and am attending church again."

Crystal's dream will take on more meaning for you if you read the three angels' messages of Revelation 14:6-12. The verses immediately following their highly compressed communiqués make it very clear that these angels bring God's last message of mercy and warning to the world before Jesus comes. These messages culminate with the beautiful words, "Here is the patience of the saints, here are those who keep the commandments of God and the faith of Jesus" (Revelation 14:12). This is the very experience these messages are designed to produce in the hearts of those who receive them.

❧ ❧ ❧ ❧

Pastor Miroslav Kis [pronounced Keesh] was a student in Ukraine when it was part of the Soviet Union. His public school teacher, knowing that Miroslav was a Sabbath-keeping Christian, ordered him to come to school the next Saturday. Miroslav went home and told his mother about his predicament. She said, "My son, I cannot tell you what to do. If I were to tell you not to go to school, I would be accused of brainwashing you, of teaching religious propaganda, and you might be removed from our home, and I would be sent to prison. You have gone to church for eight years and have learned what the Bible teaches about God's holy law. You know what my convictions are, but you must make your decision based on your own faith and devotion to God. Like Daniel, you must stand up for yourself."

That Sabbath he was in church. Miroslav had the prayer support of all the church, and felt secure. On Sunday Miroslav approached his second grade classmates for the homework assignments given out the day before. But the teacher had strictly forbidden them to help Miroslav. The boy perceived the teacher's strategy. The constitution guaranteed freedom of religion, so Miroslav could not be directly punished for going to church instead of school. However, the law did permit teachers to spank students for not doing their homework.

On Monday the teacher began to quiz the students on the assignment he had given them that Saturday. Naturally, Miroslav did not have the answers. The teacher called Miroslav to the front, and made him lie over a bench. He gave him ten sharp whacks with a stick. He did this nine times during the day (a total of 90 whacks). On the tenth time, instead of coming forward dutifully for his spanking, Miroslav, unable to endure more punishment in his frail undernourished body, ran for the door. The teacher pursued him down the street, almost catching him, but Miroslav was more agile, and escaped.

When Miroslav came home his mother recognized that he had been through some humiliating experience at school. She gave him supper and allowed him to go to bed early. Miroslav was so sore and bruised that he could not take off his clothing and was unable to rest comfortably. He awoke with a fever after a fitful night's sleep. His mother took him to the family doctor fifteen miles away. Miroslav had not yet told his mother what had happened.

The doctor examined Miroslav and asked him to take off his

jacket so he could listen to his heart, but Miroslav said, "No, I won't take my jacket off." His mother was startled and offended by his disobedience. Miroslav, looking at the doctor said, "I want my mother to leave." The doctor asked her to step outside.

Then Miroslav took off his jacket, revealing lacerations and bruises. "How did this happen?" asked the astonished doctor. Miroslav explained. "But why would your teacher beat you so unmercifully?" Miroslav explained about his Sabbath keeping and the teacher's opposition to it.

The doctor called in Miroslav's mother and in her presence peeled off the child's bloodstained clothing that was glued to his body. He applied iodine and gave tetanus and antibiotic shots. Bandaging up his patient, he said to Mrs. Kis, "Bring your boy back to me in ten days."

By Thursday Miroslav was well enough to return to school. None of the children would talk to him; he was an outcast. Sternly, his teacher said to him, "Kis, I want you in school this Saturday." He repeated this order on Friday. Miroslav's courage snapped, and he decided to go to school the next day. He went to Friday night vespers, ashamed that he had decided to transgress the Sabbath, but at the same time telling himself, "I cannot receive any more blows on my back."

His mother knew of Miroslav's decision. That night Miroslav had a dream. He saw a dark wall, against which a finger slowly wagged, a sign of warning and disapproval. Then he saw a face full of sadness come very close. Behind that face he saw wings and realized that this was a visit from his guardian angel. He knew in his dream that the angel was sad because of Miroslav's decision to break the Sabbath. Miroslav woke up and ran to his mother's bedroom. It was 1:30 in the morning. She was on her knees praying. He blurted out, "Mom, I won't go to school today, even if I die for keeping the Sabbath."

His mother lifted up her hands and said, "Thank You, Lord, for hearing my prayer." She kissed Miroslav on his forehead and said, "Go back to bed and get some sleep."

But Miroslav was fearful all that Sunday. With great appre-
hension he went to school the next day. The principal was waiting in the courtyard that morning and told all the second grade
students that they had no school that day. Tuesday morning the
principal made the same announcement. No class. Wednesday
morning all the second graders were told to go to their classroom.
Instead of seeing the teacher there, they were followed by the
principal, who looked the group over. He said, "You will not have
any class for the next two or three weeks until we find a substi-
tute teacher. My son, who was your teacher, was sentenced yesterday to three and a half years in prison because he spanked Kis.
His physician and some of your parents sued my son, and he is
to serve jail time for his offense."

When Kis was 21 and serving as a soldier back in his native
Yugoslavia, he faced court-martial, not primarily for his Sabbath
keeping, which the officers resented, but for possessing two
Bibles, which were strictly forbidden in those days of communist
control. One Bible was in Serbian and the other in Croatian. The
captain said, "For this you must face a minimum of three
months' hard labor."

On the date of his court-martial Kis entered the colonel's office
where the prosecuting captain and the jury were ready to dis-
patch this case. The faces in the room were filled with contempt
for Miroslav. The colonel looked at him and demanded, "Is it true
that you don't work on the Sabbath?"

"Yes, sir."

"Is it true that you were caught in possession of two Bibles?"

"Yes, sir."

The colonel barked, "Don't look at me with those big eyes." He
made a little dot on the wall and ordered, "Stare at that as you
talk to me."

Then the captain and the colonel started exchanging jokes that
had nothing to do with the case. About twenty minutes later, the
colonel snapped, "Kis, why don't you work on Sabbath, and why
do you read the Bible?"

He replied, "Sir, it's a question of conscience and commitment to God."

With a smirk of mock-indulgence, the colonel said, "Gentlemen of the jury, Kis has five minutes to convince us that his anticommunist behavior is not rebellion, fanaticism, or lunacy, but is indeed a question of constitutionally protected conscience. Now, Kis, just how are you going to convince us of that?"

Miroslav thought of Jesus' promise, " 'But when they deliver you up, do not worry about how or what you should speak. For it will be given to you in that hour what you should speak; for it is not you who speak, but the Spirit of your Father who speaks in you' " (Matthew 10:19, 20).

Miroslav felt impressed to tell the story of his experience in school when he was eight years of age, in all its details. As he presented his story, the five-minute restriction was completely forgotten by everyone in the room.

When Miroslav was done, the colonel rose from his seat, walked up to him and shook Miroslav's hand vigorously. He turned to the jury and said, "You are dismissed. Stay, Captain, and Private Kis."

With just the three of them left, the colonel ordered, "Captain, make sure that this man has the best life the army can offer. Kis, how many months do you have left in the army?"

"Nine months, sir."

"I want him promoted, Captain, and see that he is given no trouble. I only wish we had such faithful *communists* in this army."

Miroslav's angel spoke to him in a dream, but Miroslav's faith was no dream, no fantasy, no cunningly devised fable. There is no doubt that God uses dreams and visions to give strength, endurance, and reality to our faith.

---

1. Adapted from W. A. Spicer, *Miracles of Modern Missions*, pp. 142, 143.

# CHAPTER THIRTEEN

# "Holy, Holy, Holy"

The angels of God do not come from heaven to command our homage or control our lives but to draw us into partnership with themselves as teachers and exemplifiers of God's Word. They come especially to empower and purify our witness for Jesus. After all, angels are completely familiar with heaven, including its standards and values. We are by nature children of this earth. We need the education and guidance that angels are so well qualified to give us. Maria C., a young mother and new Christian of Charles Town, West Virginia found this out in a startling and unique way. Let's hear her tell the story:

"Awake or asleep, I've always had a vivid imagination, sometimes making it difficult for me to tell the difference between dreams and reality, at least until I wake up. Things were a bit hazy one night, as I seemed to stand in my grandfather's dining room calmly talking with my uncle. I heard someone coming down the stairs. Suddenly, out of nowhere, there were about three or four demonic creatures around me, getting right up in my face and whispering things in quiet but harsh voices. I couldn't make out what they were saying, but it was annoying and frightening. I swatted at them, but they just kept coming back.

"Feeling scared, I tried to wake up. As I opened my eyes I realized I was in bed and could see my dresser and the red light indicating that the baby monitor was on. I was relieved to awaken from the nightmare, but my relief lasted only a few seconds. Suddenly the creatures were all around me again, in my face as before, whispering what seemed to be accusations. I became so terrified that I couldn't speak, so I did the only thing I knew to do. In a silent but desperate prayer I cried to God, 'Father, please send your angels to minister to me! I'm frightened!' This prayer was strange to me. Generally, if I'm in a desperate situation, I just cry out 'God help me!' I never ask for His angels and I hardly ever use words like *minister* or *frightened*. I can only assume it was the Holy Spirit giving me utterance.

"As I said this prayer I began to roll onto my back. Suddenly, there was a bright flash and on either side of me stood an angel in brilliant splendor. A glorious light emanating from them filled the entire room. Peripherally, I could see my sleeping husband. The angels appeared to be male, though I realize that they are asexual beings. They both wore brilliant white robes tied with a cord around their midriff. They had blue sashes that came over the right shoulder, across the front and under the cord and ended just below the knee. The angel on the right was large and had blond curly hair. The one on the left was small but had the most beautiful white wings that looked soft to the touch. They didn't smile or say a word.

"I was still scared, but I didn't know if I was more frightened of the demons, who had disappeared, or the angels. In desperation I reached up for them, managing a small helpless cry. They immediately bent down and each one took a hand. As soon as I felt their hands touch mine, the angels and the fear were gone and the room, unlike my spirit, was left empty and dark.

"I lay there a few seconds wondering if I was still asleep and dreaming. Then my husband rolled over and put his arm around me. As I felt his hand on my shoulder, I realized I was fully awake. What had just taken place was real!

"What was their purpose in being there? What did I learn?

"I had been praying for humility, and I had been struggling with the issue of dancing. Not that I was big on dancing, but I did like to be-bop around the house. I couldn't understand why God wouldn't let me have some fun every now and then. I wasn't hurting anybody. As a matter of fact, I was questioning quite a few of God's standards since coming into the faith.

"I'll try to describe what being in the presence of an angel is like, but it's hard to put into words. There was a sense of awe, wonder, joy, excitement, peace, assurance, and reverent fear all wrapped up into one. Now I finally understand what the Bible means when it speaks of 'fearing' God. I came to the sudden realization that on the developmental level I wasn't much above the amoeba. Who was I to question the all-powerful Creator of the universe? I saw myself as the weak, helpless creature I am. And yet my Father loved me as His own child. He cared enough to hear my cry and respond in such a loving way. I knew that just for me He would move the heavens and the earth if it would be to my benefit. He Who controls every beat of my heart in a moment could turn His head, and I would cease to exist. Instead, He sacrificed His own Son so that I may live with Him throughout eternity.

"I came to ask myself, 'Why would I want to convulse my body to demonic beats when I could use that time and energy to glorify my wonderful Creator?' Perceiving from heaven's point of view how I had wasted my life through the years, I was ashamed. He had answered my prayer for humility in a glorious way that I could never have conceived. I was humbled to the utmost and yet felt a sense of self-worth in Christ that was far different from egotism.

"When I got up the next morning I had a nagging sense that I wasn't supposed to share this experience, at least not then. Of course, my desire was to tell everyone I knew. So, naturally, I went with the desire. First I told my husband, who said, 'Oh, yeah? That's nice,' and went on about his business. Then I told my son, who said, 'Mom, you shouldn't have told me that. Now I'll have nightmares about the demons!' I knew then that it was the Holy Spirit telling me not to share it just yet.

"I went to my bedroom and prayed. I begged the Lord to let me tell someone. I couldn't understand why He wouldn't want people to know how loving He was. But there was nothing but silence. I knew I was to trust and obey.

"My answer came the next Sabbath when I was in the presence of everyone I wanted to tell. Then I realized that if I told my story, it would have been with the attitude of "Look how privileged I am to have angels appear to *me.*" The blessing of humility I had received would have been whisked away, not by God but by disobedience, and been replaced with pride and conceit.

"I was also left with two small questions. Why were there *two* angels, and what was the significance of the blue sashes they wore?

"A few weeks later our church sponsored a seminar regarding the Sanctuary message. Imagine my delight when the speaker informed us that we do indeed have *two* attending angels—one recording angel (the smaller one with the wings, maybe?), and one guardian angel. He also told us that the blue fabric used in the sanctuary represented obedience to God's law (see Numbers 15:37-40). This is only conjecture, but perhaps angels who attend those who are obedient to God's law wear the blue sashes. Aren't those who honor God's law because of their love for Him promised a special blessing? Humbly speaking, I know I've had one.

"Now I no longer feel the need to cavort and gyrate (even in the privacy of my home) like a Baal worshiper on Mt. Carmel. Instead, it is my joy to walk in the Spirit for the purpose of serving and glorifying my Savior by living to benefit others. And that joy far surpasses the carnal thrills I used to seek. As David said,

'Thou wilt shew me the path of life: in thy presence is fulness of joy; at thy right hand there are pleasures for evermore' (Psalm 16:11, KJV).

"Also, I have concluded that the real purpose of my encounter with God's angels was not to give me an amazing story to tell others. It was to receive the message and the call they had for me—a call to abandon my resentment and joyfully live a heaven-bound life, whose influence would make a positive difference for others. Now, one year later, my husband and my son have given their hearts to Jesus, and we are walking together as a united family in the light of His gospel."

❧ ❧ ❧ ❧

Isaiah heard and saw in vision angels that cry "Holy, holy, holy" (see Isaiah 6:3). So did the apostle John (see Revelation 4:8), in a setting that shows the work of Jesus as our Savior, Intercessor, and Judge. Revelation 4 and 5 tell us that angels participate in the work of spiritually measuring our lives, not to condemn us but to reveal to us the additional growth we need in order to attain to the full stature of Christian character. See also Ezekiel 40:2-4; 43:10-12; Revelation 11:1, 2; Ephesians 4:13. God's call to holy living is always accompanied by the enabling power of His grace (see Ephesians 2:6-10 and Titus 2:11-14).

The following story reflects the subtle way God's grace sometimes steals into our lives. His grace is persistent but always polite. God calls us to holiness but never in a coercive manner. After all, if our hearts are not captivated by His love and the attractive power of truth, then what lasting good would it do us if we conformed to His ways under duress, while inwardly fuming over our high calling, as though it were some exalted form of slavery?

Patti Clifford and her parents were looking for a church. No place that they visited fully satisfied their spiritual cravings. One day, Patti's mother was sitting in the doctor's office and picked up an attractive religious magazine. Impressed by its content, she mentioned to the doctor that her family was looking for a church that faithfully teaches Bible truth. With a smile the doctor replied, "I think you'd enjoy our church. Our children like it, and I think yours might too."

"We'd like very much to visit your church," Mrs. Clifford responded.

The doctor arranged to pick up the Cliffords the following week. The church service and the Bible classes proved to be very inspirational. For several weeks the Cliffords continued attending and began to feel that at last they had found a church home where God wanted them to be. But, alas, things took a wrong turn. A few overzealous church members called and visited the Cliffords to make suggestions as to how they could improve on raising their girls, as well as improve their dress, diet, entertainment choices, and other decisions. Almost every dimension of their lives seemed to come under the scrutiny of these self-appointed lifestyle correctors. No doubt they were sincere, and in some ways right, but deplorably misguided in their approach. Patti writes:

"Finally, one day, after one of these well-meaning people left, my mother exclaimed, 'I do declare! We will have to spend eternity with people like that? Since we know what Adventists are like, there's no need ever to set foot in that church again.' I knew by the tone in my mother's voice that that was final. And I must admit that even as young as I was, I was relieved."

After another visit from a church member who felt the burden to direct the Cliffords' spiritual development, Mrs. Clifford told her husband, "I've had it! I just can't put up with this interference any longer!"

Patti continues:

" 'What we need to do is just get away for a while,' my father said. 'Why don't we pack up our tent and outdoor gear and go on a camping trip?' My mother agreed.

"My sister and I thoroughly enjoyed the long drive to the mountains. Because it was early in the season, there were no crowds. Finding an ideal camping spot, we signed in at the ranger station for Space 16. There was only one little camper trailer nearby. It occupied the space right next to us.

"The ranger had informed us that there would be a square dance that evening. My sister and I looked forward to attending. Mother went with us. Soon after we arrived, she pointed to a door near the window, gasping, 'Look at that lady!'

"Looking at her, I thought that she was pleasant-looking. I noticed that she spoke to everyone. She did not dance, but visited with several of the campers. Then she left. As I looked back at my mother, I noticed that her face had turned white and her brow was furrowed. 'That was an Adventist! I could tell. I know she was.'

"When we returned to our tent after the dance, we were surprised to find that it was the 'Adventist' camped right next to our tent. My father asked my upset mother whether she wanted to move to another campsite. 'Well, this is the best one right here by the stream, with the meadow in front. The girls are happy here. I am not going to drive all this way and have some Adventist push me out of my camp spot. We'll just pretend she's not there.'

"That seemed to work for a while. But the next evening when my mother took us to the bathhouse to wash, the woman she had decided was an Adventist walked in. Turning to us, my mother said, 'Come on, girls. Let's hurry back to the tent.'

"After we got back to the tent, my mother warned, 'Don't talk to that lady. You girls stay away from her.'

"Because we were sure that this woman must be a dangerous person or mother wouldn't talk that way about her, my sister and I did stay away from her."

Patti's father had to return to work, but arranged to rejoin the family campout on his next couple of days off. Having more than a week's supply of food on hand, Patti's mother felt confident that their needs would be met meantime. But soon after Mr. Clifford left, Mrs. Clifford became desperately sick. She was so weak she couldn't even lift her head from the pillow.

Recalling the incident, Patti says, "Calling us to her, Mother said, 'Girls, I'm really sick, and there's no way to get hold of Daddy. You'll have to go over to that lady's trailer and ask for help.'

" 'Oh! No!' we both responded in unison. But because Mother insisted, we went next door and stood there, staring at the door. 'You knock,' I told my sister. She stammered, 'No, you do it.'

"While we were trying to decide who would knock, the woman opened the door. She had the most beautiful face with the loveliest smile. At once I lost my fear, quickly telling her about our sick mother.

"The woman opened her door wide. 'Oh, come right in!'

"She fed us lunch while she prepared broth for Mother. As soon as the broth was ready, she took it over to our tent. After Mother had sipped as much of the broth as she could, the woman bathed her in order to get her fever down. Then, taking us back to her trailer, she read us stories from a book written by 'Uncle Arthur.' At bedtime we returned to our tent, telling Mother all about what had taken place.

"Mother sighed as she said, 'Well, here we go again. Anyhow, there's nothing we can do about it.'

"When Father came back, he realized instantly that Mother needed care. He was so alarmed that he didn't even take time to pack the camping gear. Piling the three of us in the car, he drove down the hill to the hospital. In the car, after telling Father what had happened, Mother said, 'You know, maybe we were wrong about the Adventists. Maybe they aren't all alike after all. This lady didn't say a word when she saw what kind of food we had or what kind of clothes the girls were wearing. She didn't even mention seeing the three of us at the square dance. She just came over to help us. We really owe her a lot. If there are people like that in the Adventist church, maybe we should consider going back to it.'

"Father said, 'I've been thinking the same thing. I'll look that lady up when I go back to pick up our camping gear. It sounds as though she's the kind of person we'd like to know. Anyway, I want to thank her for all that she did for you three while I was away.' "

Mr. Clifford returned for the gear and was sorry to see that the little camper next to their tent was gone. So on the way out of the park he asked the ranger for the name and address of the lady who was camped right next to his family in Space 15. Looking puzzled, the ranger said, "You must be mistaken, mister. Spaces 15 and 17 have been empty all summer. Nobody was camped next to you."

To straighten out the confusion Mr. Clifford and the ranger went back to their site which had all the evidence of their recent encampment in Space 16—flattened grass, recently doused campfire, and refuse in the garbage can. But the space right next to theirs, where the lady's camper had been, showed no signs of having been occupied for months. The grass was tall and green, without any tracks or signs of wear. The Clifford girls and their father stood there speechless.

"But I assure you," Mr. Clifford declared, "that lady was camped right there in the spot next to ours."

"Oh, but it couldn't be," the ranger countered. "No one has been camped there all summer."

Patti finishes her story with these words:

"Months later, in Sabbath School, I learned this verse found in Hebrews 13:2: 'Be not forgetful to entertain strangers: for thereby some have entertained angels unawares' (KJV). I wondered whether *we* had been entertained by an angel, rather than entertaining an angel ourselves."[1]

Now isn't that an amazing story? And a sad one. What a pity that we poor mortals so often act with a zeal not according to knowledge. How many times have we misrepresented our Lord by our heavy-handed witness?

God calls us to holy living. His Word instructs us to live "as obedient children, not conforming yourselves to the former lusts, in your ignorance; but as He who called you is holy, you also be holy in all your conduct, because it is written, *'Be holy, for I am holy'* " (1 Peter 1:14-16). The difference between God's approach and our meddlesome methods is as far apart as heaven is from earth. Let's learn from the angels how to be winsome ambassadors for Christ.

---

1. Adapted from "Angel in a Camper," by Patti Clifford as told to Ruth Ella Elkins, *Adventist Review*, November 15, 1979.

## CHAPTER FOURTEEN

# In Future Glory With the Angels

Scripture tells us that sights, sounds, and experiences far beyond human powers of description and imagination await the redeemed. " *'Eye has not seen, nor ear heard, nor have entered into the heart of man the things which God has prepared for those who love Him'* " (1 Corinthians 2:9). Our limited, earthbound senses make it impossible for us to more than dimly grasp the boundless glories beyond this age.

In the hereafter, all that was lost by sin will be restored. Right now our world trembles with the wounds of war, the defacement of nature through human exploitation and carelessness, and the ravages of earthquake, fire, flood, and storm. And the most unsettling force of all is human injustice—prejudice, bigotry, and violence. All these hostile forces have made our world a place of pain and woe.

But it was not always so. When the world was young, God pronounced it very good (see Genesis 1:31). It was His Creation, the product of His perfect mind and power. But sin, brought on by Satan and embraced by our first parents, disrupted the perfection of God's original order and thrust desolation into the very heart of human experience. Humanity embarked on a strange alliance with Satan. But the whole Bible from beginning to end tells us of God's plan to uproot the power and presence of sin from the universe through His plan of salvation. God's angels have been deeply involved in this plan from its start, and will continue to be involved till the day of final victory.

That is why one of our chief delights in future glory will be our friendship with these heavenly helpers. In vision, Zechariah heard God promise Joshua, Israel's high priest, who represents all redeemed people, " 'If you will walk in My ways, and if you will keep My command, . . . I will give you places to walk among these who stand here' " (Zechariah 3:7).

Because this scene was set in God's sanctuary, His operational headquarters, we can readily determine that the ones standing by were the angels who serve God day and night in His presence, and run divinely appointed errands between heaven and earth for our benefit.

This special face-to-face fellowship with angels will begin the very day of Christ's return. Jesus will send forth His heavenly messengers to greet the redeemed whom He awakens from the grave and glorifies with the living saints. Imagine the thrill of rising through the air with these winged friends who so often have cheered us in our lonely hours, braced us in times of trial, protected us in times of danger, comforted us in times of bereavement, and instructed us in our days of searching and doubt. We will not lack for subjects of discussion as we travel to heaven with these angels. And the greatest subject of all in our conversation with them will be the mysteries and marvels of our Savior's love as revealed in the plan of salvation. It is this theme that grips the interest of the angels (see 1 Peter 1:10-12). Throughout eternity, redeemed humanity and the angels who have had so much to do with drawing us to the Savior and keeping us close to Him, will marvel and glory over the plan of salvation. (See Revelation 5:11-14; 7:9-15.)

Throughout their ministry for us on earth angels have been communicators of God's truth. No doubt they will continue in that capacity in heaven and on the earth made new. With the veil parted between the past, present, and future we will be able to clearly see how, with skill and love, the angels worked behind the scenes of our lives every day to bring us to God and guide us into understanding and doing His will. Every rustle of their wings and every whisper of their voices declares His glory and conveys the music of divine love. Every influence and interposition of angels working on our behalf is directed to magnify the cross of Jesus and illuminate our hearts with the boundless glories of redeeming love.

Through Satan's crafty deceptions, heaven was depopulated of one third of the angels. Imagine the loyal angels' grief over their lost and rebellious companions who once loved the Lord and delighted in serving Him. Their grief is assuaged at the thought that the vacancies left in heaven by their former companions will be filled by the earth's redeemed millions, transformed from rebels to eternally loyal and grateful subjects of God's kingdom.

Today the angels hide their names from us and keep their identity muted. They do not wish to overwhelm us with the glory that they possess as a gift from Christ. In the hereafter we will know their names and be charmed by the striking individuality of each noble, selfless servant of God. But we shall never make the mistake of worshiping them or letting our admiration for them eclipse our love for Jesus.

Heaven's greatest light will not flash from angels' wings nor glint from crowns of victory the saints will wear, but will shine from the places where Christ bore the wounds of Calvary for us. Habakkuk, seeing Christ in a heavenly vision of future glory, records, "He has rays flashing from His hands and side, and there is the hiding of His power" (Habakkuk 3:4, NASB). It is the power of love, the power of grace, the power of mercy that Satan's darkest waves of rage were powerless to quench. For God's love is stronger than death and the grave, mightier than any foe who would stand between our souls and the Saviour.

For this reason the science of redemption is the greatest of all sciences. The redeemed, the unfallen angels, and worlds that never sinned will join together in studying the inexhaustible theme of God's self-sacrificing love, as displayed on Calvary, and in all heaven's benevolent deeds on behalf of fallen humanity. The hearts of all the ransomed will thrill with ever-expanding devotion to the Lamb. To heaven's angels, the reward for their labors over the past six thousand years will be the satisfaction of having worked in effective partnership with God for the salvation of human beings who will now be their companions for all eternity.

Stacey C. a teenager from Wichita, Kansas, said it well: "One main thing I look forward to in heaven is the joy of meeting my angel and thanking him for all his hard work in leading me to Christ. Right now I just want to learn how to listen to my angel and to the Holy Spirit, so that I can do God's will and help others the way I should. I don't want all of God's unselfish work for me to go to waste." That's a good philosophy of life, isn't it? One to which all the angels of heaven can join their voices in saying, "Amen!"

# Who Are the Angels?
## A BIBLE STUDY

So many theories exist regarding the identity, origin, and activities of angels. The truth about angels is far more beautiful than the best of human imagination could create. So, let's see what the Bible has to say about angels.

### Origin

Angels are divine beings created by Christ. See Psalm 145:2, 5; Colossians 1:16.

They are not self-existent or self-sustaining, but derive all their power and life from Christ. See Hebrews 1:1-4.

They existed before the creation of our world and humanity. See Job 38:4-7; Genesis 3:24.

### Nature

They are spirits subject to God's authority. See Hebrews 1:7, 14; 1 Peter 3:22.

Angels have physical forms made of heavenly

substance. See Ezekiel 10:12; 1 Corinthians 15:44-46.

They are not human beings, but are of a higher order. See Psalm 8:4, 5; Hebrews 2:2, 7.

Their nature differs from ours. See Hebrews 2:14-17.

They are mighty, powerful, glorious beings. See Psalm 103:4; 2 Thessalonians 1:7.

Angels obey God's commandments. See Psalm 103:20.

Like human beings, they have freedom of choice to obey or disobey God. See 1 Peter 1:12; Jude 6.

They can travel between heaven and earth infinitely faster than the speed of light. See Daniel 9:21-23; John 1:51.

Human beings do not become heavenly angels at death or under any circumstances. See Luke 20:34-36.

In their work on earth angels sometimes appear as human beings. See Genesis 19:1-11; Mark 16:5-7; compare with Matthew 28:2-7; Hebrews 13:2.

There are different orders of angels: seraphim, cherubim, and other unspecified orders. See Isaiah 6:1-4; Ezekiel 1; 10; Revelation 5:11.

Their supreme commander is Michael, the archangel. See Revelation 12:9.

## Population and Habitat

Their home is in heaven—specifically, God's sanctuary. See Psalm 80:1; 99:1; Isaiah 6:1-4.

They stand in God's presence and have direct access to Him at all times. See Luke 1:19; Matthew 18:10.

They are dispatched to all parts of the universe, particularly to our world. See Psalm 68:17; John 1:51.

Angels are innumerable. See Daniel 7:10; Hebrews 12:22.

One third of them rebelled and are now called devils; they are banished to this earth and no longer have access to heaven. See Revelation 12:9-17; Jude 6; 2 Peter 2:4.

## Work and Interests

Heaven's angels are deeply interested in our salvation and the means of its accomplishment through Christ. See Luke 15:10; 1 Peter 1:10-12.

Angels are God's messengers. See Psalm 103:19-21.

Angels know our names, addresses, and occupations. See Acts 10:1-6.

Angels give instruction to God's people. See Judges 13:3-14; Acts 7:53.

Angels are deeply involved with helping God's people preach the gospel. See Acts 5:17-21; 8:26; Revelation 14:6.

They are deeply connected with the work of building up and guiding God's church. See Acts 10; Revelation 2, 3.

God uses angels as ministers of justice. See Numbers 22:22-35; 2 Kings 19:35; Daniel 4:14-17, 31-33; Revelation 15:1; 16.

Angels guide, direct, protect, and provide for God's servants. See 1 Kings 19:5-7; 2 Kings 1:3, 15; Psalm 34:7; 91:11; Acts 27:23.

They intervene in world affairs, holding back destructive forces, restraining tyrants, and punishing evil. See Daniel 10:10-14; Acts 12:20-24; Revelation 7:1-4.

Each person has a guardian angel. See Matthew 18:10.

Angels are witnesses in God's work of judgment. See Daniel 7:9-11; Revelation 5:8-14.

Angels are involved in the sealing of God's people. See Revelation 7:1-3.

Angels refuse to be worshiped, but they worship God. See Revelation 19:10; 22:8, 9; Hebrews 1:6.

They will all accompany Christ at His return and gather the redeemed from all parts of the earth, separating the wicked from the righteous. See Matthew 13:39, 49; 24:30, 31.

Angels will be among our closest companions in heaven. See Zechariah 3:7.

If you enjoyed this book, you'll enjoy these as well:

**In the Presence of Angels**
*E. Lonnie Melashenko* and *Tim Crosby*. A contemporary collection
of encounters with angels from Voice of Prophecy listeners.
0-8163-1261-3. Paperback. US$10.99, Cdn$15.99.

**An Angel's Touch**
*Nathalie Ladner-Bischoff*. Stories of miraculous intervention and
angels at work in our world today—showing that miracles still
happen. Each story will make angels seem more real and build
faith in God's never-ending love.
0-8163-1577-9. Paperback. US$8.99, Cdn$12.99.

**It Must Have Been An Angel**
*Marjorie Lewis Lloyd*. This inspiring classic contains true stories
selected on the basis that the outcome has no logical explanation
other than divine help. 0-8163-0363-0. Paperback. US$6.99,
Cdn$9.99

**Angels**
*Ellen G. White*. Turn to any page in this precious collection of
quotes to find comfort and enlightenment about the selfless love of
heaven's messengers.
0-8163-1310-5. US$5.99, Cdn$8.49.

Order from your ABC by calling **1-800-765-6955**, or get online
and shop our virtual store at **www.adventistbookcenter.com**.
> Read a chapter from your favorite book
> Order online
> Sign up for e-mail notices on new products